'A LITTLE THING CALLED L OVE'

By

Rebecca Clark

"A Journey Through Alzheimer Disease"

ISBN: 1-4033-5400-6 (e-book)
ISBN: 1-4033-5401-4 (Paperback)

Library of Congress Control Number: 2002093276

This book is printed on acid free paper.

Printed in the United States of America
Bloomington, IN

1stBooks – rev. 09/13/02

This book is dedicated in honor of my mother and to
my husband, Larry,
Without his understanding support and love I would
not have been
able to take this journey with mom

Acknowledgements

I would like to thank all the kind, dedicated people
who helped
Mother and me on our journey through Alzheimer's
Disease.
My heartfelt thanks to:
Wilma, Connie, and all the wonderful people I met
through
the local Alzheimer Support Group,
Bunni and her staff at Elderly Day Services,
Carolee and staff at Kandiyohi County Family Service,
The personnel of the Rice Hospice Program,
The Doctors and Nurses who cared for Mother.
Words can never express my gratitude to all our
friends and family
who gave their loving support through actions and
prayers. A very special
thank you to Diane and Bev for their unselfish
devotion to mom and me.

It wasn't like I woke up one morning to find my life suddenly different. There had been signs. No, she didn't suddenly become ill, not suddenly a different person. But with one early morning phone call my worst fears were realized... the fear that my strong, confident mother really wasn't infallible and immortal. There really was something drastically wrong. Oh, my God, not my mother!

On this hot morning in July 1995, I listened as the doctor told me that the tests showed probable Alzheimer's disease. The urge to close the words out was strong. I wanted to run but I had to listen and try to grasp what I didn't want to hear.

Oh, yes, my world would be forever different, but first I had to run, and yell, and scream and cry.

I had always believed someone as loving and giving, as she had been all her life, would live a rich, full life until God called her Home.

Not my Mother! How would she deal with this devastating news? So many times, after returning from visiting nursing homes, she had said that she hoped she would never get that insidious disease. Now, I had to tell her the very thing she dreaded was very possibly, a reality.

The doctor and I discussed 'if' and 'when' she should be told. Due to the constant pain of Trigeminal Neuralgia and the recent robbery of her home, the doctor feared this once very optimistic lady would suffer from depression if she were to find out at this time. She had been exhibiting signs of depression, although she always denied it, so I agreed we wouldn't tell her yet. An appointment was set up with the Neurologist who would follow her case. We agreed to tell mother that the new doctor was to help evaluate her Trigeminal Neuralgia. Perhaps the Neurologist would have a gentle way of telling her. At least I would have three weeks to get her used to the idea that she could have Alzheimer's disease.

As I hung up the telephone the tears began to flow. I ran. I screamed. I cried.

Since my father had died in May of 1992, I was looking after her. I was the one of six children living closest to her. During the intervening years since then I had noticed our roles were gradually changing. I was becoming the parent of my parent. Our relationship had transpired from a deep bond of friendship and enjoying the wisdom of my mother, to taking care of her bookkeeping, banking, and keeping her busy schedule straight for her. She would call me at work to ask me to stop at her last place of purchase to sign the check. Occasionally, she would write two checks for the same item. Sometimes the amount was written out on the 'pay to the order of' line. Now, she was asking me to balance her checkbook as she was becoming frustrated with the task at hand. I found this odd … she was the one who taught me and had always found my errors in the past. Soon she was having me write the information on the checks for her and then I would show her where to sign. As more late fees appeared from previous month's transactions, I began to mail her bills for her. Later, I would find them stamped, sealed ready to mail, tucked neatly between drinking glasses in the cupboard, behind the mixer on the counter and sometimes even in her recipe box. Luckily, when we had to remove Dad's name from their joint checking account, we had the foresight to put my name on the account with hers.

Mom had continued to stay active with her various interests, church work, Girl Scouting, and other volunteer positions, after Dad's death. Sometime, late in 1994, I began getting occasional telephone calls asking if mother was ill, as she had forgotten a meeting she was scheduled to attend. It wasn't normal for her to forget anything.

She called me at work more often, wanting to find out what day it was, where she had put something, or to discuss a telephone conversation she had just finished.

Mom had been missing Dad more as the winter rolled in, so I figured she was just lonely. She always told me she was glad I was the one who lived closest, because of all the children; I was the most like Dad. Like my father, I could calm her anxieties. It made sense to me that she would be calling me more.

New Years Eve mother and two of my nieces came to my home for a party. Both girls informed me that their grandma had driven through two stoplights on the way over. I dismissed it.

Mom always picked up two ladies for Sunday church services; and after services the three of them would dine together before she took them home. Upon arriving home, she would always call to tell me what a delightful lunch they had together. One particular Sunday, Mom was in church without her ladies. When questioned where they were, she embarrassingly told me she had forgotten to pick them up. In our telephone conversation that evening she admitted she had gotten lost on her way home from church. I really didn't think too much about it – O.K. – so her mind was preoccupied on the drive home. I didn't realize it then, but this was actually a common occurrence.

In May 1995, my friends' son was confirmed. I helped her with the food and setting up the tables. We realized we needed another large platter. Mother was planning to attend so I called her about 12:30p.m. to ask if she would bring one of her platters when she came. She said "yes" and that she would be there right away. She never showed up. Mom had been to their house many times; she was like a 'Grandma' to these kids and certainly knew the route. Where was she??? I called her house. Maybe she was still there. No answer. I called several more times to no avail. Finally, I called her neighbor and asked him to go and check if she was home. Maybe she had fallen and gotten hurt. He told me he saw her driving away about 1:00 p.m. but hadn't seen her return. I sent Larry, my husband, to search the streets in the area to try to find her. He came back alone. I went to search for her at some of her friend's homes, but couldn't find her. She had to be hurt somewhere! She would have called me! I drove to her home searching the ditches along the way. No Mom! I let myself into her house to call the police; it had been four and a half hours since I had spoken to her. I was scared! The frightening thought that something was drastically wrong had me near hysteria. As I reached for the telephone her car pulled in the driveway. RELIEF!! She was all right, just shaken up over her stupidity [her word] at getting lost. She had grabbed the platter and left for town right after

I called her. Once in town, she could not remember which street Patty lived on; she had driven up and down the streets looking for the familiar house. Remembering there was a telephone in the grocery store, she stopped to call me but couldn't remember the phone number. She started to look in the telephone book for the number, then realized she had forgotten Patty's last name. Back in the car, she drove around unfamiliar streets. When she arrived home, she informed me that she had become so confused that when she did finally find herself on a familiar road, she just followed it back home. *"So, here I am!"* She was so apologetic for letting me down.

After that, she would contact me before every Deacon visit to let me know she "was going exploring". [The Deacon's responsibility is to visit shut-ins, sick or elderly members of the church.] I would always know the address of her destination. I would know where to start looking - just in case. Outwardly, she maintained her sense of humor about this, even though it scarred her.

The signs were there. I had just not wanted to see them.

I only knew a little about Alzheimer's disease at that time, enough to know that the affected person becomes someone totally different as time passes. They may become belligerent, tactless and cruel and experience personality changes. Eventually, they will become as infants and die without mind function, totally oblivious to any stimuli. Picturing my beautiful, gentle mother this way was totally repulsive to me.

Mother and I were about to embark on quite an adventure. Together we would learn a lot about this Alzheimer Disease and its effects on the dementia patient, the caregivers and loved ones who choose to 'hang in there' for the duration.

The most important thing we learned at that time was – just because a person is diagnosed with probable Alzheimer's does not mean they instantly become a no-brained- nothing. I would highly recommend that if you are close to someone who suffers from Alzheimer's you learn as much as you can about this disease.

Attend support groups for Alzheimer's and other related dementias. Books and pamphlets are helpful guides to tell you what to expect, and in mapping a rough idea of the progression of stages...but realize that each case is different. There are no set-in-stone, neat columns of detailed information. Stages overlap; incidents occur for a day or so, they may never happen again, or they may disappear for a few months before reoccurring. Support groups are real people living with the disease right now. This is where we found our greatest help.

The progression of Alzheimer's disease can only roughly be mapped out. The different stages were developed as a guideline of what to expect at roughly what point. I believe it was developed for all us folk who think we have to know exactly when 'this' or 'that' will happen, so we can schedule our lives. Believe me there is no set schedule for the progression of Alzheimer disease, so get ready... you <u>will</u> learn time really means nothing.

Learn to let go. Let go of the idea that your loved one will always be his/her perfect self. Let go of the image that you are the child he/she the parent. Let go of the ideological way you thought he/she would finish life's race. Let go of nearly everything worldly that you always thought so important.

Keep your sense of humor very close. If you don't have one, find one! Find humor in all the sadness. I don't mean tell-a-funny-joke-humor; I mean humor that comes from every day experiences if you just slow down enough to recognize it. For example, after one seemingly long morning of trying to redirect my little Mama from destructive behavior, she finally sat quietly to write in her diary. I seized the opportunity to escape into the newspaper. After awhile, Mom asked, "What are you doing?"

"I'm reading the paper," I replied.

"Well, what are you reading?"

"Right now I'm reading the obituaries.*"*

"Oh! Well, am I in there?" she questioned.

"No," I replied.

"Are you in there?" she quarried.

"No," I chuckled.

"Well that's good," she smiled, *"I'd hate to be here alone."*

When we would shop, I would usually fill out all the information on the check then hand it to her for her signature. By writing all of the information ahead of time before she signed, it helped her continue to feel important and maintain her dignity. Once I asked her to sign her 'John Henry' on the signature line, and she did – 'John Henry' was written just as neat as could be!

One day we stopped at my house to pick up something I had forgotten. I asked mom if she wanted to come in. *"No, I'll just sit here,"* *she answered.* A few minutes later I returned to find her slumped down in the seat and was pulling the seat belt over her head. She couldn't figure out how to unhook the seatbelt, but was able to loosen it enough to slide it over her head. I asked what she was doing.

"Well, I'm getting out of this!"

"Why?" I quizzed, "I thought you wanted to sit there."

"Well, I don't know. *She told me to get out,"* she said as she pointed out the open car door. Following her lead, I saw my black lab sitting by the door.

So, you see, humor is good! Try to see the humor in all situations, before you react negatively. At least try to see the situation through that persons' eye.

Another thing I learned - that would make life a little easier for the caregiver is – watch the moon and sky. All of us are, in someway, even minutely, affected by a full moon. Imagine how a person with dementia can be affected. Several days around a 'full' or 'new' moon, behaviors become worse. Confusion that isn't so prevalent the rest of the month is totally visible. '**Sun downing**' is what the experts' call the "anxious pacing time" that gets increasingly worse as the disease progresses. 'Sun downing' usually happens as the sun begins to set-hence the name sun downing. This is also very common on cloudy, overcast days. Summer months my husband, Larry, would call to check on mothers' mood. If it was a sunny day and she was irritable and anxious, he would not cut his hay crop that day. Invariably, it would rain even if the weatherman had predicted dry weather. Her moods were also "right on" for predicting snowstorms in the winter.

The last bits of wisdom I will mention are: learn **not** to correct mistakes in their conversations or actions, and remember their reality isn't always the same as yours. In fact, as time passes, their reality is generally always different from yours. Whatever it is, it is real to them. So don't argue.

Take a moment to imagine how it would feel to not know who you are. To realize that at one moment – you are a vibrant, energetic, viable person involved in an important activity, in the next, unfamiliar faces surround you. At this point, you feel overwhelmed, confused and frightened as you try to comprehend why these people, who are total strangers, are talking to you as though you've been dear friends all your life. Suddenly, the fog lifts and you are laughing and talking with your friends, yet totally unaware that only moments earlier you didn't have the foggiest notion who they were.

Mother was born and raised on a farm in eastern Iowa. She was a beautiful person, inside and out, valuing God, family, honesty, integrity, education and manners. On Saturday, May 31, 1947, surrounded by her loving family she was united in marriage to Birk Lowther. Their union was blessed with six children: Kathy, Becky, Steven, Susan, Bill, and Jeanne. In 1957 Dad moved our family 300 miles away from mothers' hometown to southwestern Minnesota. This was the first major move mother ever made. Having lived within a few miles of all her relatives for 35 years, you might imagine how difficult this move was for her. The second and final move they made was 120 miles farther north in 1969. She was not one to wait for strangers to offer the hand of friendship; she would introduce herself to all she met with her warm easy manner. She gave of herself to others her entire life. She saw the good in everyone, encouraging them to use their God-given-talents and to reach their fullest potential by believing in themselves and in God. Like her parents and grandparents, Mom was a college graduate, a teacher, and very active in her church and the communities where she lived.

Writing in a diary began when she was very young and continued in some form until Christmas 1999. When my father died in 1992, she wrote to him frequently to ease her loneliness. My siblings and I grew up hearing stories of our parent's lives. Both our parents had written down the stories of their childhood so we would always have them and can pass the stories accurately to future generations. How thankful I am to have learned so much of my mothers' past. That knowledge helped me fit into her memories throughout the disease, except for one period of time when I was her sister. Mother was the only girl; her five brothers were Don, Ken, Clyde, Bruce and Fletcher. You will see references to 'Sister Betty' or 'Sis' in her writings, but this person is my father's youngest sister, Betty, who married mothers' youngest brother, Fletcher.

When we first moved to Minnesota we lived in a tiny apartment in town for a short time, otherwise mother had always lived in the country. Mom and Dad raised horses, cats, dogs and of course, their children. We had one foster sister, Kay, half brother, Jim, and many other young persons that my parents took under their wings. We were also involved in the raising and training of horses, and were active in Girl Scouts, Boy Scouts, 4-H and of course, church. There was never a dull moment at our home.

Mothers' writings from her journals combined with my journaling and narrative will help me convey our experiences as we journeyed together through her disease.

As you read the exerts from her diaries you may feel the frustration she had with the disease, and with herself, for not having control of her thoughts and for feeling she had lost her worth as a human being. You will feel the lost-ness as she gropes with finding her thoughts. You may more fully understand the disconnectedness she felt as she tries to follow her thoughts from beginning to end. I will begin with excerpts from her letters to my father in 1994. This will help illustrate how the dementia affected mom before it became apparent to me that something was wrong.

June 15,1994

Good Morning my Beloved! I just had to go to the basement to get a pail and the clothes from the dryer – but – I must have gone up to the third step when I realized I was going to do something else- perhaps you will remember that the older we get the more time we spend thinking and trying to figure out "the what am I hereafter!" Thinking that I only had gone up one step, I stepped backwards. Unfortunately I must have been up on the third one at least. Consequently I was thrown off my balance and stumbled backward trying to regain my balance when I was on the floor. I hit my right shoulder against the furnace- scolding myself for my stupidity and/or ignorance, I managed to get up and come upstairs. What damage did I do? Well, I could bend my fingers so figured I hadn't broken anything- I thought!! Every once in a while I'm reminded that I have quite a few bruises of this fall. I really must have gone through quite a few contortions in trying to avoid the fall- The cement floor and furnace just didn't give a bit!!! The cast will be on 6 weeks, I guess. I suppose the kids will decide I'm becoming incompetent—

Oct.21, 1994

My Dearest Love, I'm at Jeanne's home this week. How I wish you were here with me really—Why am I at Jeanne's? Well, Jeanne and Guy are in Toronto attending training for their church. They left one day before yesterday (10-11-94) and will be back late Sunday night the 16th.

Dec. 30,1994 – 3:20a.m.

Good Morning my Beloved- Yes, it is too early to be up but I've been awake for a while. Countless and varied thoughts have been going through my head. Foremost are my memories that we have shared over the years. And now we are about to enter another new year. Once it was May 3,1992 and our Lord called you Home. Now May 3,1993 and May 3,1994 are past history. Yes, I am still in our home with no immediate plans for leaving it.—Well, my Precious Love, it's an hour later- 4:20a.m. And I've regained my sense of well- being and identity with you again. This seems to be a communication link with you that gives me a renewal of our life together. I am so very very grateful that the Lord drew your path to Iowa. Happy 1995 New Year, My Precious One. Just think this is our 48th New Year. Until we meet again my deepest love to you- and thank you for watching over us- I love you very very much.

On January 25,1995 mother was diagnosed with Trigeminal Neuralgia, a disorder of the trigeminal nerve. This presents as episodes of severe, stabbing pains that affect the cheek, lips, gums, or chin on one side of the face. Simply touching the face or talking can trigger pain so intense that the sufferer is unable to do anything during the duration of the attack. During this period of time, the doctor was weaning her off different medications she had taken for years, hoping that her confusion was caused by the medications, not dementia. We opted to use acupuncture to keep from adding a new medication to control the pain. One of my sisters in Minneapolis saw an acupuncturist for migraine headaches. Mother would periodically spend a week with her while she had the treatments on her face. After a few treatments this did control the pain quite well. We noticed that when the pain was the greatest her level of confusion was also elevated.

On July 5,1995 mother returned home from church to find her door broken in and her belongings strewn about the house. She had been robbed; felt violated and afraid. I was out of town until evening the day of the break-in, and her inability to reach me only added to her fear. She called the police and her minister who came to her aid. The minister helped with the police report and stayed with her until I arrived. Early the next morning she had tests scheduled at the U of M to help determine the likelihood of Alzheimer's disease. How could this emotionally traumatized woman possibly be able to concentrate on her testing?

When she was finished with the testing, mother reported to me that she had "wasted her morning playing children's games". She couldn't understand what earthly good those games might be to a doctor. To mother the tests were just a "bunch of silly nonsense".

The Trigeminal pain and the robbery would be enough to cause depression and confusion in any 72-year-old person. I hoped these were the culprits, even though I did suspect something more serious.

Sunday morning- Aug. 12,1995 (I think)

The last couple of times I've left here for Minneapolis I have the feeling I'm running away from our home and it bothers me. Yes, there are times I'm uneasy as a result of the robbery. I just feel that I need to be here long enough to feel my home is mine again and that no one can push me out of it.—I feel an unsettledness much of the time when I'm here alone anymore and I don't like the feeling. This is our home and I can't let some hood push me out of it!!!

Aug.20, 1995

I sort of suspect that the kids may have encouraged Deanna to move here. I do believe they think I'm really aging. I'm sure you remember how often you used to encourage me to cut back on some of these meetings. Well, I've done it! However, now that I don't have a scheduled day everyday I have trouble keeping track of what day is what. Wouldn't be surprised if the kids think or expect me to become quite incompetent as I age. But that is a natural part of aging!!! How I wish I could see you and hear your voice saying, "I love my beautiful Mama". This I do know, my Precious Husband- You are waiting for me to come to you and I shall when the Lord calls my name- I do know we will be reunited in Heaven and share a new life together again.

Rebecca Clark

Sept.6, 1995

A cloudy day mostly my Dearest Precious Love! How I miss you!! I had an appointment with my doctor this morning for my physical. I must have seen him earlier this year because he had this neurologist from Minneapolis come out and check me over. With summer coming to an end, I realized that I hadn't had a good check-up yet as my doctor had always done. He will record the results of the tests and send them to me. He is retiring later this year- I will miss him- He's always been so thorough and practical. No one knows better than you that I have been slowing down- Yes, I realize I'm getting older. The neurologist tests this summer showed some loss of memory. Doc told me to stay involved. Actually I have been pulling back from some activities. On the way home from the Deacons meeting last night I had decided to resign from the Deacon Board. My term is over this year so I guess I'll stick it out. He also told me to read the daily paper more carefully and thoroughly, to read more—keep my mind active—Actually I have been doing a lot more reading of books and articles than I have taken the time before- plus stay active! A couple of weeks ago I had decided that I wasn't slipping as much as I could when I consider my year. First I'm widowed- the worst of it was living alone and missing you. You always enabled me to do my Girl Scout work and volunteer work and very important was the interest you always showed in whatever I was doing. We did make quite a pair, didn't we?! I still thank God that He brought our lives together. We can be justified of the family we produced also.

Deanna is living with me this year and possibly the next two years. She's a senior in H.S. now and wants to go to college here. I know it is really nice to have someone in the house with me. [At this point of her letter mom tells of all the activities of the rest of her family, and that she will go to church for quilting the next day before going back to her report on her doctor visit. Deanna is my sister Jeanne's oldest daughter and mothers' first granddaughter.]

The doctor told us (Becky went with me today) that there is a Dr. here in the clinic that is able to treat this Trigeminal Neuralgia and that I should see him when it flares up again. Becky had planned on taking me into the cities for acupuncture next week. So we will have to talk about that. It would be simpler than making the trip to Mpls. again.

Sept. 7, 1995

Good Morning My Love! I must say it is good to hear someone in the house again. I'm not the only one here. It is also good to have someone to cook for again. Best of all- I just don't feel so alone now. First frost of the Season is possible tonight in the North- It may be a long winter or we may be due for a beautiful "Indian Summer".

Monday, Sept. 18, 1995

Good Morning, My Love! I'm home again after 4 more days of treatment with the acupuncturist. At least this time I'm not quite sure just how much help I got this time. He helped my left leg but I have not been

17

pain free this time except for 2 days- maybe 3- last week while I was at Susan's home. I can't tell you what a blessed relief it is to be pain free even for a short time. Yesterday morning I woke up at 4a.m. with intense pain. Sometimes the pain lessens after I get up and move around – apparently the blood circulates more when I'm moving around. I really do enjoy having Deanna here. The house is no longer so lonely- consequently I'm not either. She is good company and a good worker. I must also say, I really like having someone to cook for again. I was so pleased when Jerry asked me Friday if they were coming to the farm for Sunday dinner yesterday.

Earlier this year when Larry mowed the yard and pasture he said I owed him a lemon pie- so when I got up at 4a.m. I did it! I had made rolls on Sat. only the 2nd time, I think since you've been gone. I hadn't made a lemon pie for many years. Kathy reminded me that I always made lemon pie for you. I still owe Larry another one. These trips to Minneapolis cut down on some of my time.

These are times when I must admit to myself that it would have been quicker to stay with the M.D. and let them cure this Trigeminal Neuralgia by severing the facial nerves but that is so drastic! As a result I'm still trying to tolerate it as a bad nuisance. However, in all honesty these are times when it seems easier to "toss in the towel!"

Yes, my Dearest One, there are also times when I so long to be with you, but somehow I must make sure that our loved ones understand that Death is not an end- it only opens the door to a new life with our Lord and our Loved Ones who have preceded us. I do not really know what style of life we will live when we leave this home but I do know it will be in Heaven with you all. Just to see you again, to be a family again- in God's Kingdom!

I must go on. I'm determined that I can't let myself get depressed. I must keep looking ahead to fulfillment of coming Home to you and my Lord and parents and grandparents.

I've definitely found out that things go better for me after I've "talked" with you. My deepest love to you, my Precious One- Until next time. Mama Betty

Oct 14,1995 - Saturday morning - 5:15a.m.

Good Morning My Love, I know it is too early to be up but sleep eludes me. As usual my thoughts turn to you and our life together. It seems like such a waste of time to lie in bed awake with idle thoughts. So, I will talk with you for a while.

Yesterday was Friday the 13th. Of course that reminded me of Dad because he was the suspicious one. Mainly he would not start a new job or project on that day. He would procrastinate himself around it and Mom would always consider it a waste of good time.

Becky and Patty came out yesterday and did my house cleaning. My how the windows shine! Yes, your wife has gotten to the age or stage where she can't do some of these things. Becky still helps Patty with things like wallpapering, and then I'm the recipient when they come out as a team and do things that are really beyond me.

This has been a different year for me. Yes, I do have quite constant reminders that I am aging- but I have no regrets because "time passing" brings me closer to our reunion. I miss you so very very much – but I do try very hard not to dwell on what can't be helped. I become more aware of the fact that I'm so very grateful that Grandma A. and Dad were instrumental in teaching me to be a positive thinker. I do have so much to be grateful for. We had a wonderful life together, didn't we? And I do look forward to our reunion in God's Kingdom.

Yes, I'm actually feeling better today. Strangely enough it is due to acupuncture. This Trigeminal Neuralgia is such a pain so much of the time but the treatments have made it tolerable. I still don't like the pain but I cope. Mainly, it affects my eating but it hasn't reflected itself in too much weight loss yet. The mornings are the worst. Brushing my teeth can make me cry if I let it. Eating is difficult because I can only chew on the left side of my mouth. The numerous pressure points that precipitate the pain stay active and alert- It is aggravating that I must accept the fact that if I touch my right side of my face that I set the pain off. Yes, it leaves eventually so I try to remember to keep my hand away from my face. I remember that Dad used to have some type of neuralgia that would cause him lots of pain. I wonder if this is the same. Maybe that was why he had the wish to go to Davenport and learn to be a chiropractor when he was younger. I also think of Susan with her migraine headaches. When I was her doctor he told us we both had the identical pain lines. I do hope she doesn't have to experience this.

Speaking of Susan, she and Matt are coming out here this Wed. night – will stay overnight and then take me to Des Moines to see Fletcher and Betty. I'm so glad Deanna is with me. It is so nice to have her in the house. She is busy with school plus her job. Last night was the first time since starting school that she allowed herself the luxury of just watching TV. She usually is in her room studying. She keeps a full schedule- Just looked at my watch- Now 6a.m. Also seems like I'm getting sleepy- actually, I've relaxed by writing to you. I don't have any fantasy that this is a two-way conversation with you, Beloved, but I do know that it seems to keep alive my link with you and for a time anyway it bridges the gap. In no way does it replace our time together- reminds me of the times we'd lie in bed and just visit about things.

I'll have a lot more to add after I come back from Iowa. I'm so glad that Jeanne and the kids will be here with Deanna. I think it will be good for them also.

Farewell for this morning my Precious One. I am doing better now. Becky is also making me walk at the Mall several times a week to get me in better shape. Being inactive isn't good for anyone for any period of time. Walking on the road as we did isn't so easy anymore. This big farm machinery is as wide as the road and very large and long.

Oops- sounds like a windy day ahead! My love is yours always and forever. That wind reminds me of snow. They did say yesterday that we could get the first snow during the night.

Dick put these new heat controls on the furnace several weeks ago and it makes such a difference- the heat is constant and steady.

I send you all my love and I will pick up the reins again to carry on until we meet again, never to be separated, in our Lord" timing. I covet your prayers, my Love, at times I envy you because you are with our larger family. All my love always and forever—

Sunday Oct. 15,1995

'My Special friend.' A friend is one who stays closer than a brother or sister, which is as it should be. However my "friend" stays much too close to suit me at times. Her name is "Trigeminal Neuralga". She has been my constant companion now for several years! Since 1995 she has been my constant companion and always at meal times. I have discovered that she will leave me alone if I pay attention only to her. She doesn't bother me if I don't talk too much or too long or if I do not drink cold water. I have learned to tolerate her friendship if I do my part – talk as little as possible. If I find I must eat some food I chew only on one side of my mouth very carefully and talk very little. This morning I've taken my medicine and eaten my cereal. Big Deal!?! Yes, actually it is! Drinking cold water to take my medicine reminds me very effectively that Trigeminal Neuralgia is very much a part of my life. Cold water really turns the pain in my face to high gear. But I must swallow the pills with some water and I must concentrate in order to remember to chew only on the left side of my mouth or else the pain is excruciating. Breakfast is

over – time to brush my teeth - Another ordeal! Is there a way to eliminate this daily ordeal? Oh, yes, it's simple – have the doctor severe my facial nerves to be freed from my friend. But I don't consider this a proper solution. Severing the facial nerves would leave me a horrible sight. I would no doubt go off by myself to avoid all human contact!!! Susie did tell me about acupuncture like she has used for her migraine headaches that I so generously endowed her with. I don't really understand it but it works and I accept it!

Christmas Eve Day 1995 Morning

Good Morning, My Dearest One-Yes, it has been some time since I've 'talked' to you. But always remember you are always in my heart and thoughts.

Christmas is a little more poignant to me this morning; it seems it must be because I'm missing you more. Christmas was always so special to us-probably because it was the timing of our making our commitment to be always together and marriage was the first step that bound us so closely together.

So often I think of how blessed we were to find each other- no, that the Lord chose to put us together.

We both came from strong solid families, which is a blessing in itself. Of course Christmas was always so special because it was Jesus' birthday added to the fact that it was also Mother's birthday and Grandma always made so much of her 'babies' birthday. I'm so glad you got to know my grandparents. They were special people weren't they?

Your Mother had died at such an impressive age for you, and you had always missed her so much. I know that becoming enmeshed in our family you found solace and healing as a complete member of a family unit. It is still mind boggling to me when I reminisce and realize how easily our lives blended together. This reminds me again of Fanny Greer when she insisted that our marriage was made in heaven. Fanny, a spinster, had never known the joy of marriage but she recognized a good one!

I have enjoyed having Deanna living with me. Yes, it is different in the way that after being alone for several years it was an adjustment to having someone in the house again. That is a blessing in itself. She looks after me so well and sees that I eat properly. Yes, there are times when it would be easier not to eat but she insists and I realize that she is right.

Well, this is the Day before Christmas. We will go to church at10:00 then come home and load the packages in the car and the food and drive up to Sue and Dons'. They are the hosts this year again.

Becky and Dan came out yesterday and took me shopping for a new dress. I guess it has been long enough that I really thought it was time that I could afford one and, yes, I felt I really needed to wear something different.

Actually when I got up earlier I went in to take my shower but I thought of you again and decided I needed to talk to you.

Fletcher has been very ill for 3-4 weeks now from viral infection. He has shown some improvement but the Dr. says the longer he can keep him alive the better his chance of recovery. Yes, My Love, your little sister, Betty, has been having a difficult time these past weeks but it sounds like she's doing O.K. I must call her today. Reg is with his mother this weekend. That will be a real boost for her. Her neighbors from Manchester have really been good to her and helping where possible. She sounds good on the phone but it has been a difficult time to be alone. Her pastor and church friends have been very supportive also. I may go down after he comes home from the hospital so she can get back to work; as she said, "we have no money coming in at all now".

I just looked at my watch so I'd better get my shower and get dressed for church. After church we will be going to Sue and Don's for dinner. Tonight we will go to Steve's church then at Susies home on Christmas Day.

How I wish you could be here—I miss you so much at times. It appears that the next few days will be that time. Thank you for listening to me "Daddy".

I love you, Mama Betty

New Years Day 1996

Happy New Year, my Dearest One. It's a white frosty day-snow and frost covered trees. I've just spent about ½ hour talking to Clyde. This is the second time he has called me about Fletcher. I just realized that I haven't talked to you yet about Fletcher. He has been hospitalized since Dec 6 and is so ill. Clyde had just talked to Betty and seemed very depressed. Fletcher just doesn't seem to be able to throw off the infection. Poor Sis is in the roughest spot in her life but bless her heart she is showing great strength. I offered to go to

Des Moines to be with her. She wants me to come when Fletch gets out of the hospital. Clyde just told me that she had to stop talking because she was crying. Things are not good today! Oh, how my heart goes out to her-she must feel so alone. Reggie spent last week with her. I can imagine the aloneness she felt when he left to go back to Mpls. I feel so helpless! And I must admit I just am not ready to lose my baby brother and neither is Clyde. Yes our family is dwindling away. But, oh! How I thank God for memories of days past. Also the older I get the more I value and appreciate my heritage.

As usual, you are helping and supporting me. I was pretty much a basket case when I hung up the phone. My next wish was to be able to talk with you-so here I am- I do miss you so very, very much. So many thoughts race through my mind and I feel so helpless. I will go to Des Moines when Betty agrees. But she doesn't want to impose on me until Fletch can go home. Yes, my Precious One, your little sister is having a rough time but she seems to be doing quite well. Living doesn't get easier, but then, at my age how can I expect it to?!

I must say that taking the 'Writing Your Memories' class was one of the best things we could have done. I trust it will prove to be a blessing to our children. Also I find that my benefit was finding that it also helps me. Not only was it a project we could do together, it was a project we both enjoyed and in your physical absence from us the writing to you like this is a panacea, a source of comfort for me. When I'm writing to you I feel a sense of connection and you are as close to me as my heart. So, my Love, as I write this morning, you are giving me the strength and encouragement to continue on. Oh, how I miss "our" talks. How I look forward to our Reunion in God's Kingdom!!!

"Talking" with you has been a big help again. However, I must confess my feelings of apprehension are not really leaving me yet. I think both Clyde and I are beginning to wonder if he will make it. They still have him on Morphine.

Thank you for your patience with me through our years together. I am, oh, so thankful that the Lord chose to have our paths cross and merge our families together. You still have your magic touch of settling me down, of making my problems understandable and most of all bearable. I so appreciate the warm comfortable feeling that enfolds me now. I was setting up for a big cry after talking to Clyde, but thanks for being my sounding "board" as usual.

Jan. 1996

Called Betty- He's about the same- no real change. Reg is coming down Friday to stay the duration. I will ride down with him. He gets weaker and weaker. Oh, my little brother, what can I do for you? How can I help you? I know God is keeping you in His Providential care- I'm just not ready to give you up. So many of our loved ones are with you already. You will have a royal welcome into God's Kingdom. Yes, I know we are each in God's hands to do His bidding. Gracious and merciful Father of us all, I commit my little brother into Thy loving care. I feel so helpless. Am I strong enough to see him- to lose him? Yes, my Lord, I know he will be freed from all earthly cares when you call him Home. How can I selfishly cling to his earthly body when I know he will only find true life in your kingdom?

At Des Moines with Fletcher and Betty—Jan.1996

Dear God and Father of us all, I come to you on behalf of my baby brother, Fletcher. Since I got word of his illness it has become more difficult for me daily. You see we nearly lost him in the fall of 1937. At this time, Mother had been ill for some time. She had been at Finley Hospital in Dubuque for quite a long time. Don and Ken were in charge of things at home as Dad spent time with mother when he could. When Mom was so ill, I learned to do all the cooking, including baking 15 loaves of bread every Saturday. Dad and my 5 brothers plus an occasional hired hand could eat a lot of food, especially fresh baked bread hot from the oven.

Living on the farm we had the usual dairy cattle, hogs, and a big garden. So we canned and preserved everything we could for winter. As I recall there was usually 400 qt. of meat and garden produce canned and on the shelf in the basement. I definitely remember going to the basement at regular intervals to help or to help sprout the potatoes in the winter. If they were allowed to grow sprouts they would become soft and mushy. No, I did not like doing that job at all. I suppose we all had to take turns doing it. The truck from the creamery stopped regularly to pick up the cream, leave butter and feed that Dad had ordered for the cattle and hogs. We didn't have a refrigerator so the butter was kept cold by putting it in a cream can that stood in the cold water tank. I suppose we also put other food in that can also. The tank was in the pump house where the Delco Plant was. At this time we had electricity but many people did not. The Delco Plant provided ours until the time R.E.A. lines came through the countryside. Grandpa also had his own Delco plant for electricity. Grandpa also had running water in the house, so when I stayed with them I loved taking a bath in their tub. We used the washtub for bathes at our place- so it was a treat to stay with the grandparents. Besides I got to play with our cousins and I dearly loved being with my grandparents.

Our world was temporarily shattered on a fall day in 1937. Mother was in the hospital at Dubuque, IA. Dad and Ken were picking corn. Our neighbor had picked their children and Bruce and Fletcher up at Joseph School then picked me up. We were always excited getting home from another day at school. As usual, when the driver stopped in front of our home both Bruce and Fletcher bounded from the car in a race to see who could get the funny paper first from the mailbox. Just as the boys got out of the car a large truck carrying huge logs drove by. As I came around the back of the car I saw my baby brother, Fletcher, lying on the ground in a pool of blood. Forgetting that I was wearing my first new coat, I picked Fletcher up off the road, clutching him to my heart. He was bleeding so much. The trucker stopped. I told him Dad was in the cornfield just down the hill. So he ran down to get him. Ken ran to the garage to get the car as Dad took Fletch from my arms, got in the car and off they raced to the hospital at Monticello. It seemed like hours before dad and Ken got home from the *hospital. Of course Fletch stayed in the hospital and dad went back to him after he knew we were O.K. I really don't remember how long Fletcher was in the hospital but it seemed like a long time. The frightening thing was that I could see that one of Fletcher's eyes seemed to be pushed out of place and I knew he would lose his sight. The highway Patrolman stopped at our house the next afternoon to get names and information about the accident. Dad and I rode to the hospital with him. I was afraid to see him again because I knew one eye was gone. The patrolman picked me up, carried me into Fletchers' room, giving me time to really look at my baby brother. His little head covered with white bandages- I couldn't see either eye- just bandages! I was so relieved to know that his eye would be all right soon. When mother heard about her baby being hurt, she demanded that she be allowed to go to her baby at Monticello. So she was transferred there, determined to stay, which she did. In due time both our patients were able to come home. Our family was again complete! In due time both Mom and Fletcher made a good recovery. Now, with Fletcher's Home Going, they are again reunited- never again to be separated. Perhaps I envy them!!*

Mothers' youngest brother, Fletcher, died in January of 1996. She was able to sit with Fletcher at the hospital before he passed. By his bed she wrote- *"As I've aged going through many phases of life, I have concluded that life's experiences are ultimately good and many can be used to advantage- because we learn new lessons and confidences in ourselves and our lives. Net result- a deeper faith in God- He is adequate for our needs."*

The morning of his funeral I was wakened by soft sobbing coming from my mother lying beside me. I turned to her and encouraged her to let the tears flow. She could not really cry. In all my years I had never seen her cry, not even when my father died. Tears would well up in her eyes but never come. This early morning I encouraged her to cry, let the tears come. "Don't hold them back." To this day I hold the conversation that followed in awe and amazement of what the mind can do.

My mother's voice changed to that of a young girl as she told me, I *"would not allow her to cry."* "Why not?" I questioned. She said I had *"punished her unfairly for breaking the vase."* Realizing I was no longer me but someone else in her mind I probed, "What vase dear, I honestly don't remember".

"The wedding gift to you and daddy that fell off the shelf and shattered when I ran into the room behind Kenneth and Clyde," she said holding back her tears.

Now, knowing I was her mother in her mind I said, "I'm sorry dear, I don't remember the incident, but I must have disciplined all three of you children for an accident that really was no one's fault." "I am so sorry."

Indignantly she retorted, *"No, you only blamed me and when I cried you told me to stop. You said crying meant I was guilty."* After a moments pause and in a quiet voice she said, *"Mommy, I'm sorry. I didn't mean to cry, but I didn't break the vase."*

I had to think fast. What do I do or say now? I got up and walked around to her side of the bed, knelt down and cradled her face in my hands. Looking into her sad eyes I said, "Please, dear daughter, forgive me for being so unfair to you. Forgive me for hurting you, my precious little one. I do remember the vase being broken but I don't remember the incident. You know my quick tongue. Perhaps I reacted to the stress I've had worrying about Fletcher. Whatever the reason, I had no right to be so cruel to you. I love you, please forgive me."

"I'm sorry, Mommy, I didn't mean to cry," she said.

"No, Dear, I am sorry. You have nothing to be sorry for. You can cry. You need to cry. Tears are cleansing to the spirit. Please, forgive me for hurting you."

With that, we hugged each other and she cried, really cried, for a long time.

Later I went to get Kleenexes to dry our eyes. When I returned I was once again her daughter.

I don't believe she was ever aware that this event ever transpired. When I referred to it later in the day, she had no idea what I was talking about. I decided it was one of those healing moments our Lord allows us in some of our deepest trials. Mother was able to cry after that... and did so, freely.

This would not be the only time in her remaining years that I would be her mother in her mind, but it would be the most poignant time.

Feb.15-'96

I'm at home today- a beautiful day. Just cleaned the kitchen. Shakiness is getting worse. I don't understand this. Should I call the doctor again?

Took load of clothes down stairs- Forgot how to start the washer

Becky said an appt. in a week or so.

Dear Lord, how I wish I could understand this stage of my life. It just gets more confusing for me day by day. I keep reminding myself that I do firmly believe that all things do work together for the good for those who love the Lord and are called according to His Purpose. Am I becoming too impatient? When I got this diagnosis, I remember walking around and around the dining room table asking God- "Why me Lord," Then as if in answer I responded, "Well, why not me?!" Father in Heaven I pray for understanding and some acceptance of something-I am so grateful Lord for the family you gave me to. What a blessing it was to have been raised in a fine Christian Home. My life has been blessed in so many ways. I trust and pray that our children will be able to make the same type of statement.

Monday Night March 11,1996

Hello, my Precious Love, I decided it was time to talk to you again. Our kids were home yesterday for dinner and also a conference of things that lie ahead for my care and/or concerns. Seems like they have done a fine job of evaluating the total picture that lies ahead of me. It has been a long time since they had been home at the same time so I really appreciated their presence in addition to the future planning they have done on my behalf. They will be back on Thursday when we will go to the lawyer and get Power of Attorney and whatever notarized for legal purposes.

I am entering another period of adjustment. A neurologist checked me over and one real possibility may be Alzheimer's. I don't like the sound of that but he said there is some medication for it. What more can I expect? Now that I am 72 years in a couple of weeks, what more can I expect. I do hope and pray that I won't make life too busy and hectic for Becky if this develops.

I spent all day March 22 at the hospital. Started the morning with a MRI. I was in that tube for a long time. I think Becky said 1-2 hours. Then I had quite a number of X-rays before I could leave. Haven't gotten any results yet, so waiting is the name of the game! I really miss you in times like these. You could always make a questionable situation sound better. But your Becky is remarkably like you in this respect.

March 15,1996 Fri. A.M.

I do not mean to be a cantankerous old lady. Again, I wake up with my mind teeming with questions. I'm sure I'm not senile yet!! But, I figure it must be that my total inexperience with always being dictated to about money has left me in a questionable and vulnerable position. God help me. I do not believe I am beyond the capability of learning and being able to function. Have I erred so much? Am I now a puppet with no responsibility? It seems that I am again relegated to the same inferior attitude that I was kept in when your Dad was alive. Am I feeling sorry for myself? In a sense I suppose I am. Have I been ineffective in the things I've done? But I wake up this morning feeling just pretty inadequate for any good use. For many years I've felt adequate and secure with my Lord that I have been accepting of the feeling that whatsoever state I am in therewith to be content. Why, Lord, am I beginning to wonder and question just where and what my role is from now on? I need your help and understanding. Perhaps events are happening too fast for me.

April 9, 1996 – Good Morning, My Beloved,

Oh, how I miss you! Life is getting more difficult day by day. I saw a new doctor yesterday. I'm with a woman doctor again. She made a good first impression anyway. Honestly, her questions, etc. just give more evidence of the truth that Betty is aging, forgetful, losing contact with reality and God knows what else. Oh, how I miss you and the talking we used to do. I could always count on you to keep me steady and in touch with reality. You kept me on that balance beam! I am very grateful Becky is so close- but I could see yesterday that I am already becoming a burden to her. How quickly I'm entering "old age of dependency"! I believe I must accept the fact that from now on life doesn't improve- it only deteriorates. The only advantage is that I will be reunited with you sooner. I am afraid I will be a burden to Becky and Larry. Their intentions are so good but they also need their own life style. I do pray that the Lord will enable me to keep my spirits up and consequently more alert and less of a burden. Honey, pray for me that I will not become too much of a burden to Becky and the rest. Kathy was home last week during Spring Break. The girls cleaned the cupboards for Spring-cleaning. I loved having them here. Loneliness was not here that day.

April 9, 1996

My Dearest Friend and Husband, How I wish you were here with me right now. I need your level head. I just asked Becky how many years you have been with our Lord and the parents who have preceded us. So for 5 years I can say things and life have gone on as before. Yes, our family continues to grow and mature. They are doing well. Deanna has blessed my life while living with me. She and Becky are my caretakers.

Apparently February 25, 1997, Mom reread her diary as she added under her entry of March 15, 1996 this comment; *Little did I know when I wrote the preceding page or comprehend what lay ahead of me, of the many adjustments that will have to be made. What a difference a day makes in any given time. I really don't or can't comprehend because I've never been close to an Alzheimer's patient. To me it seems like such a contrast too much of my life. For once I'll have to face each day for what it brings. I know I won't like the accompanying confusion. Plus I've never liked being a burden to anyone especially my loved ones. Because of my age and the absence of my precious husband, the burden will fall on Becky and Deanna, the ones who live the closest. Also I've never used my tongue as a weapon of defense to my knowledge. I really don't know how I will cope. I hope I will gain greater understanding along the path that lies ahead. Yesterday was my first full day alone. To my knowledge things went O.K. So far, no one has said anything differently. I am becoming more and more grateful that the Cognex medication was developed at the precise time I developed this. I accept each day for what it brings and trust my Lord for His sustaining care. Completed Feb.25, 1997*

Many times after Moms' 'probable' Alzheimer disease diagnosis, she and I would discuss her dementia. She would always question what she 'might be forgetting' and how her behavior had been. I would answer honestly. In the past, knowing 'the facts' helped her to handle situations more easily. I believed she deserved to know how the disease was progressing. Generally these discussions would begin as a result of her feeling vulnerable and attacked personally by an action or statement that had been made. Often, reminding her to take her medicine would trigger the conversation. She would question why I reminded her. Had she become *"so dimwitted"* she couldn't be trusted to remember on her own? Sometimes they would begin after being angry with Deanna and I because we wouldn't give her any time alone, or because she thought we never came to see her.

Mother was aware that she had Alzheimer disease. She would tell the people, in her various groups, that she had been given this diagnosis; she asked them to be patient with her as she explained they may have to remind her of previous conversations. She remained active in her various church groups, Bible study groups and Girl Scout activities. As long as she could remain actively involved in her meetings, we made sure she was able to attend. Mother was a very social person and covered her inabilities gracefully. So good, that many of her friends would ask me why she claimed to have dementia. For the most part, I believe Mom was on top of her thoughts.

The first couple years that the facial pain she endured, the full moon, and being over tired, caused much of the confusion she experienced, but her short-term memory was definitely affected. Many times she would not remember that her children had just been home, yet a few days later she would recall the most recent visit. Sometimes she was asked about her past career days. She was a teacher before she married my father, then she became a mother and housewife. Yet, she would reply that at one time she had worked as charge nurse in one of the local nursing homes and had done nurses aide work in other cities where she had lived. (This was what I had done much of my working career.) Other times she would say that she had been a buyer for Gorham Silver or had been Vice President of Bluebird Enterprises. (My sister, Susan, performed those jobs.) I believe this showed how deeply interested she was in her children's lives. Mothers concern for the welfare of others continued until her passing.

It became obvious, as the disease progressed how deeply engrained her faith in God was and how young she was when this faith was instilled in her. Even in the later stages of the disease, when she was pretty much unaware of what was going on around her, the prayers she lifted to God asked for mercies for all around her and especially for the families of individuals who were mentioned 'deceased' on the radio news earlier in the day. (Deanna and I decided that as long as we kept her praying, no one would detect she was into the further stages of Alzheimer's.) It amazed me that she couldn't remember from one minute to the next, yet, when she prayed at the evening meal, or before bed, she could recall the names from the morning radio obituaries and pray for their families. God and church were always important to her. She always felt her minister was a man she could confide in and receive assurance that God was in control. It bothered her at times that she felt abandoned by her minister and God. She did not realize that this was only in her mind, not in reality.

May 5, 1996

Life does not remain static!! A sudden determination to face and to accept reality certainly does change my direction.

I have known that the doctor was watching me for the possibility of Alzheimer's. I figure I will know for sure this week, Tues. However, at church this morning the light did dawn and get my attention! The tests on Tues. will tell the story. However, at church, it hit me, I am not ready to accept such news. Making a mental note I knew that I would have to talk to Sam with Becky- for the purpose of facing the reality head on. I know I hurt her a few times the other day when I made flippant remarks- not intentionally but it made me realize that perhaps my thoughts or speech would even change.

Yes, we talked to Sam. He expressed his appreciation of working with me when I was on Session and was so strong. He was aware of this prospect then and I've been off Session now for probably 6 years at least. How can one's personality change so much without my awareness? [Sam was the minister of her church.]

However in church this morning while following the bulletin and singing, if my eyes moved away from the fixed print I was at sea- having lost my space. Sitting next to me was Deanna and she noticed my quandary and guided me. So now, I'll also be a burden to Deanna as well as Becky.

At this particular point right now-2:15 p.m. Sun. May 5, I am glad I acted on impulse and that we talked to Sam. Becky, Deanna and I are now face to face with the problem. Sam says I will never lose my God but can he promise me that? I know I am a Child of God. He has controlled my life, my ways of work, etc for 74+ years now. Is it possible I could lose contact with my God? Oh, I pray that I don't! Please God keep a close rein on me. Is such a disease caused by chance of one's diet? I don't know. Thank you! I pray for strength Lord to hold out as long as I can. Can my family members possibly forgive me for hurtful things I may say to them? Lord, in your mercy, be with each and every one of us through the allotted time I may have.

I am so eternally grateful for my heritage, parents and grandparents. I think of Grandma A. dying at 90+

and such a clear mind, a beautiful person, wasn't she? What is Alzheimer's? [She begins copying from pamphlets she has about Alzheimers']

Alzheimer Disease- is a type of dementia that affects the brains' ability to think and reason. In the past, Alzheimer's and other types of mental decline among the aged were lumped together as senility. It is now recognized that there are many types of dementia and Alzheimer's is one of the more common. Although it sometimes strikes people in there 40's and 50's, it is most common among the elderly. The disease accounts for more than half of all admissions to nursing homes in the U.S. What causes it?

At one time dementia was thought to be an inevitable component of aging. Medical research has demonstrated that most older people retain their mental acuity. What causes Alzheimer's is unknown, although the disease is believed to be related to the degeneration of certain brain cells. Some recent research has suggested a viral link, but the disease itself is not infectious or contagious. It tends to run in families, suggesting a genetic association. However, not every descendant of every person who has it is afflicted. How is it treated and diagnosed? There is no test to diagnose; instead diagnosis is established on the brain of symptoms and by eliminating of causes of the mental decline. These might include stroke, hardening of the arteries, anemia, nutrition deficiency, thyroid disorder, alcoholism, infection, tumors, and the effects of certain drugs. Once these possible causes are ruled out a presumptive diagnosis is made on what is assumed to be present. Since no specific clinical test or finding is unique to Alzheimer's disease, the diagnosis must be done systematically excluding all other diseases that could be responsible for the symptoms. While there is no specific treatment for Alzheimer's itself, there are measures to help a person with the disease.

Thank you, my Lord, for the one who developed Cognex just in time to help me and others like me.

*needs controlled environment

Often, treating an underlying condition that is contributing to the mental problems brings improvement. For example, many Alzheimer patients suffer depression or delusions that compound their memory impairment, leading to a situation known as an excess disability state in which the patient is doing worse than normally would be expected. Treating the depression may bring about improvement, even though the Alzheimer's itself remains unchanged.

What can I do for myself?

Much of the burden of caring for Alzheimer's patient falls on family members. The resulting stress takes a toll on patient and caregivers alike. Consider getting some assistance for everyone who is involved either by hiring someone to care for the patient while the family takes a break and/or obtaining some form of family counseling. If care is being provided at home, modifying the environment can reduce certain stresses for both the patient and the caregiver. Keep the home uncluttered to improve safety as much as possible. Be sure needed objects are always kept in the same place, is the patient does not need to learn anything new. Doors and windows should be locked to avoid wandering. Patients should wear an identification bracelet, indicating condition, name, address and phone number. Be patient and recognize that when the patient seems stubborn and combative, it is brain damage and not contrariness that is causing the problem. As the disease progresses, the person needs increasing help and support in performing simple tasks.

Symptoms

Impaired intellectual function and memory loss

Combative Personality disturbances, including apathy, withdrawal, agitation, irritability, and quarrelsomeness

Increasing confusion and disorientation

Changes in self-care, such as an inability to dress appropriately or tend to personal

Grooming

Wandering away

Erratic moods

Loss of bowel and bladder control

Is Alzheimer's disease dangerous? It is invariably fatal unless the patient dies from another illness before the disease reaches the final stage.

What can I do to avoid Alzheimer's disease? There is no means if prevention. Elderly people can guard against developing symptoms that mimic Alzheimer's by eating a well-balanced diet, getting regular exercise and attending promptly to any problems with hearing, eyesight or other conditions.

The course of Alzheimer disease usually progresses slowly, with intellectual and emotional capacity gradually diminishing over a period of 2-8 years.

Progression of the disease is characterized by the person's increasing withdrawal from responsibility and social contact. <u>*In time, physical health also declines.*</u>
[AMA Home Medical Encyclopedia page 19]
<u>*Alzheimer's Disease*</u> *Sunday afternoon- May 5, 1996*

A progressive condition in which nerve cells degenerate in the brain and the brain substance shrinks. It is the single most common cause of dementia. Alzheimer's is responsible for 75% of all dementia cases in those 65 and older. Originally classified as a "presenile" dementia. Causes unknown. Is now known to be responsible for 75% of dementia cases. Info on Alzheimer's increasing and expanding in recent years. The progress of the disease, which in most cases represents several years of intellectual and personal decline until death. <u>*Cannot be arrested.*</u>

Causes- unknown- but number of theories- A reduced level of acetylcholine and other brain chemicals in people with Alzheimer". More common in people with Down's Syndrome- Occasionally a common pattern of inheritance, one affected parent may have a 50% chance of inheriting the disease. Incidence- Onset rare before age 60- increases steadily with age- up to 30% of people over age of 85 are affected.

3 broad stages—

#1- patient notices his/her increasing forgetfulness and may try to compensate by writing lists or by soliciting help of others. Problems with memory often

cause the patient to feel anxious and depressed. These symptoms sometimes go unnoticed.

At this point mother ended her copying of the facts she found on Alzheimer's disease. To complete the information of the next two broad stages, I will continue to quote from the same medical encyclopedia she was using.

#2- Forgetfulness gradually shades into a second phases of severe memory loss, particularly for recent years. They also become disoriented as to time and place. Their concentration and ability to calculate numbers declines and dysphasia is noticeable. Anxiety increases, mood changes are sudden and unpredictable, and personality changes soon become apparent.

#3- Patients become severely disoriented and confused. They also may suffer from symptoms of psychosis, such as hallucinations and paranoid delusions. Signs of nervous system disease begin to emerge, such as primitive reflexes and incontinence of urine and feces. Some patients become demanding, unpleasant, and sometimes violent, and lose all awareness of social norms. Some become docile and somewhat helpless. They neglect personal hygiene and may wander purposelessly.

Monday A.M. May 7, 1996

Deanna has gone to school. I just put my laundry in the machine. Becky will be taking me to Mpls. tomorrow- May 8th- for more testing. Only you, O

Lord, know what the path ahead will lead to. The reading from the Medical Books I read yesterday seemed to prove to me beyond a shadow of doubt, the diagnosis will be Alzheimer's- like it or not. Talking with Deanna last night was an eye opener but it also was overwhelming. First the fact that she and Ryan who helped her and had accumulated actual Alzheimer brochures telling about the disease- I will read and try to assimilate the material today.

When I realized yesterday at church that I wasn't ready for this diagnosis, I asked Becky to go with me to talk to Sam. She did. It was a time and a day to have my eyes opened. I don't believe I've ever looked at myself to point out weaknesses before. But now it seems that (to me, anyway) the more understanding I gain of what to expect, of what is actually happening, that just maybe I can retain a part of the life around me for a time, at least.

As I was walking across the floor as I came upstairs, the thought that went through my head was- Birk hasn't lived here since 1992- but now "Betty" as I've known her doesn't live here anymore either!!! Will I be able to stay in familiar surroundings? Precious Lord, Sam assured me that you will never let me go. I am so very, very grateful for my heritage. Born and raised and baptized in the Reformed Presbyterian Church of Hopkinton, IA into a wonderful family. I had 5 brothers but no sisters.

Time out... must eat my breakfast and take medicine. I wonder if writing things down will be help or a hindrance. I have accepted, at this point, that change is all around me just waiting for the opportunity to slip in. From the time Mother got so ill in the 1930's I've always seemed to be in control of a situation- BUT! Now I know I won't experience that freedom again. Precious Lord, I need Thee every hour more than ever. I shall hope to be able to walk and talk with you when you call me Home. May it be at a point before my actions or works will alienate me from my precious family. I pray you can direct me in spite of the Alzheimer's. Surround my caregivers with the accumulated love through the years. Since you've been "Home" my husband, I've cherished the wonderful memories we had shared together. I pray that there will be some good memories left for our children to share.

The Bible verse that Grandma A. and Dad (Earle) impressed so firmly in my mind is there this morning- 'I have learned that whatsoever state I am in, therewith to be content'

Will this insidious disease remove this from my mind and heart? There is another verse, I've always believed- 'all things work together for the good of the Lord and those who are called according to His purpose. (I realize I just mixed up some of the wording) another mistake!! Forgive me, my Precious Ones. I am of mixed emotions writing my thoughts. I'm not doing this to hurt you, but I feel compelled to try and hang on to some of the things- events, or whatever that might be a 'sign of the past' that I can reread and gain something from in the future. Now I will stop for now- 9:12 A.M.

Rebecca Clark

Tuesday, May 7ʰ, 1996

Becky takes me to the Univ. of MN today for more testing. I was greatly relieved and relaxed when Dr. Mary Sullivan met me. She is the same specialist that tested me a year ago. The testing is tiresome but apparently she learns a great deal about the inner me that I don't understand. We must have worked on this for a minimum of 6 hours. Right now it all seems like child's play but apparently Dr. Sullivan will advise my doctor of any changes she finds.

Wednesday- May 8,1996

A cloudy dull day- I'm alone but Becky may be coming out sometime. Deanna is at school. I don't know if she works tonight or not but time will tell. Her graduation draws closer.
*This is the day the Lord has made, I will rejoice and be glad in it. I will rejoice and be glad in it. I will face this day with courage and be sustained by faith. I will face this day knowing Your Grace is sufficient for the day. Lord Jesus, I thank you for your presence with us this day. Amen
I have taken my medicine, eaten my bowl of cereal. The Redstarts ate their breakfast at the same time. I do enjoy these birds. Now I am sitting in Grandpa's rocker. I am so glad to have this rocker as well as Grandma's rocker in my bedroom. Hopefully they may serve as an anchor for me to cling to as changes take place. These grandparents are my distant past and they both meant so much to me. Because I was the only girl with 5 brothers and we lived on Ridge Farm

20 miles away at Hopkinton and very young, I spent most of my summer in Cascade with my maternal grandparents. Brother Kenneth also went along the first year to keep up with his active sister- a big help for Grandma. Grandpa was 6' tall. Grandma was 5'. She could actually stand under his extended arm. One of my favorite memories was in 1935, the year they celebrated their Golden Anniversary. Grandpa usually milked 4 maybe 5 cows, Gurney cows. Their milk was so rich and yellow. When Grandpa came in from milking Grandma would put the milk from this one cow into the pantry, to sour or congeal for what she called clabber. No, I can't say that I liked it but I did eat it because she asked me to. Usually the next morning she would take 3 sauce bowls to the pantry, return to the table with 3 bowls of clabber. She sprinkled either brown sugar or white sugar on top of it. We ate this for breakfast. No, I didn't like it but I wouldn't disappoint my Grandma. I was 13 years old at the time so I got to help with all the festivities. It was a wonderful summer of celebration. Probably my favorite memory of this time was the morning of the anniversary- when

Grandpa came in from milking he went directly to Grandma and folded his big arms around her wishing her a Happy Anniversary, telling her how happy he was to share those 50 years together were the best possible and he loved every minute of it. He especially liked her feather-light baking powder biscuits. I loved my Grandma so much but there are 2 foods I eat for her but have never eaten for anyone else. That is clabber, the sour milk I mentioned earlier, and the other was dandelion greens. You'd better believe that her yard didn't have any dandelions in her front yard when I went from my visit there. I especially remember Grandma taking what she called her dandelion knife plus a smaller paring knife and we went to the front yard. Of course the root of the dandelion goes straight down into the ground. She taught me how to stick the point of the paring knife into the soil so as to sever the root of the dandelion as I pulled the severed part up out of the ground. The next step was to pick up the greens, take them to the pump, wash them thoroughly, and then they were cooked for dinner or supper. Served with some vinegar seasoning. Again, I ate those greens (I preferred the beet tops actually) but I never ate any dandelion greens for anyone else. Stubborn wasn't I?! One of the reasons that I loved being with my grandparents was that I had my own room- my own bed! You see with 5 brothers in a smaller 3-bedroom farm home, I did not have my own room. My bed was a narrow cot in the living room adjacent to Mom and Dad's bedroom. But, when I was at Grandma's I had a big bed. A Birds Eye Maple bed. So that was the beginning of my love for Birds Eye. I had my own little closet also. I had to stoop over to go through the door but I could hang my clothes up in there and use 2 shelves.

May 8, 1996

Appointment with Dr. Mary Sullivan- U. of M. Testing to determine any changes from testing a year ago. It was a long day. I was delighted to see the same Dr. as I had a year ago. I recognized her and she thought that was excellent and encouraging. I had forgotten that this was what I called playing games a year ago. Now I would say they were games for a specific diagnosis whether it be Alzheimer's or something else. But I do hope there will be specific answers this time. My reaction right now, 1 P.M., May 8'96- No, I do not like the idea of Alzheimer's because of the subsequent changes to be expected and probably not understood, to be forgotten later, perhaps never to be remembered. It seems like the pattern in my life has always been- if I can only understand how this works, then I will be able to roll with the punches. I so hope to get enough information about this strange disease to at least understand enough to be able to roll with the punches, if possible.

Gracious Lord, I do firmly believe that you will never give us more problems than the strength you have given us to cope with it. No, I don't understand why it is necessary for me to have this experience, but I do believe you have a purpose for my good. I do pray for understanding of the disease. Yes, my Lord, I so dread becoming a 'nothing' or something less than I am or was destined to be. One of my most earnest prayers will always be that as the changes materialize that you will keep control of my tongue so that I don't say things that will be especially hurtful to my loved ones. I must accept the fact that the time will come when I am no longer in control of anything. I suppose I will become more and more the child as time goes by. Will I forget or lose my precious heritage? Will I be able to realize it if I do? Yes, I do hate living in a void like this seems to be shaping up into. Do not let me harm any of my family members. I love each of them to the utmost of my capability.

My testing—all are timed
#1 She reads a story, I am to repeat what she read
#2 She gives me a series of numbers to be repeated
#3 Putting one flat-sided peg in holes with one flat side
 only
  Removing peg from box replace in adjacent box
#4 Identifying pictures of various objects or things

First she had me use my right hand the next time she had me use my left hand. I've always figured that I was disgustingly right handed but!! It took less time using my left hand than with my right hand! Could I have originally been intended to be left-handed but was forced to use my right hand? Not that I ever remember and I do not remember any emphasis on my brothers regarding this. It will be interesting to hear if she made any particular comment on this. I believe there were 2 timed events that showed me faster with the left hand.

It was a long afternoon with much duplication it seemed but I noticed the difference in my reactions. I don't know how these things are diagnosed or what they teach her for my benefit or behavior. Somehow I get the feeling several times that I performed more quickly than I had a year ago. I believe the doctor said there is a medicine that can slow the progress of Alzheimer's, but it is very expensive. I don't know if our health insurance would cover the expense or not. But if it would work and slow the progress during the summer so I could be relatively normal of like I have been, personality wise, I would surely appreciate it as I see my family when we visit them. Hopefully I will not change too rapidly

.

May 9,1996—

Bev called last night- is picking me up for Circle meeting this afternoon. I'm of mixed emotions on this but I do know that I just can't dig a hole and put myself into it. Please Lord be with me each step of the way. With your help and help from family and friends I hope and pray I won't be too much of a burden for anyone of the family. Yes, today will be my first test among friends who have seen some of these changes but didn't say anything to me about them. I realize that each day of my life will see more changes. I do pray that I will be able to accept these changes. I am of mixed emotions realizing I've been given a death sentence. Thank you, Precious Lord, for your presence with me and with those I love. I need Thee every hour, more and more. Also please be with my loved ones giving them strength to walk this path with me. I know I cannot do it alone. I still wonder why those friends and family that recognized the changes did not say anything to me about them. I realize it probably couldn't have made any difference anyway. But friends are friends, aren't they?

I just got home from Circle. I had a good day. I even made a common sense statement during the meeting, though I don't remember now what I said. Yes, I am glad I went. Well, that is one hurdle over. I pray that I may always be of some service to my Lord in some way that is pleasing to Him. I must remember that I am serving our Lord when I am praying for others. My children will also need their Mother's prayers on their behalf. They will suffer through this as I do. I only wish it were possible for them to be spared the heartache.

May 10,1996—

Another cloudy gloomy day. Becky will be out to take me to my hair appointment and shopping. Oh, how I hate to be a bother! The sad part is it will only get worse. I keep wondering why me? Now I understand why not me?! I do not look at my situation as a punishment. I can only accept the fact that God has some purpose to work out in our lives. Dear Lord, I pray for continued strength as well as much understanding of my situation so as to lessen the strain on my children- especially Becky and Deanna who will have the majority of the responsibility

May11,1996—
I've been up for awhile- It has taken me awhile to figure out what day it is for sure. I had awakened Deanna for school; but it is Saturday. So, this is confusion!! Oh, my Precious Lord, I do not like this way of life you've set me on or allowed me to pursue. But I do love you, my Lord and I trust you. I pray that you will not give me more than I can cope with. I'm sure you won't, but I'm also aware that things are different or will be changing from now on. I dread the prospects of the future that lies ahead of us, for my loved ones are also involved. This fact hurts the most of all. I don't want to be a burden to them. But I know

my independence is going up in smoke. I will be digressing to more of a childlike state. Help me, my Lord, to cope with all this. The sun is out now – must take my medicine and eat my breakfast. Thank you, Lord for loving me.

May 14 – Tuesday—

Another new day faces me. What will I do with it? Will I remember much about the day? It is raining. Has been a cold wet Spring and no sun this morning-just rain. Am I being selfish by wanting to stay in my home as long as I can? Is it possible that I could be more normal and manageable if I do stay here? This is the home Birk built for our family and us and it is familiar to me. I think it would also be easier for Becky if she continues to insist on being my caregiver. The part that bothers me is becoming a burden to my loved ones.

When Becky and I came home from the testing in Minneapolis I decided to quit driving the car. I just don't want to be involved in an accident or to kill someone.

(Thankfully, this was Mothers decision and not one that we had to make. She was still mentally capable of operating a motorized vehicle, but she feared that she could be the cause or be involved in an accident. She would not be able to forgive herself had this happened. Because she was aware that she was getting lost while driving, she didn't want to get so disoriented that we wouldn't find her. As time passed she would often regret her decision to give up driving as it took her freedom to come and go as she pleased.

Her decision also conflicted with her desire to stay somewhat independent of her caregivers.)

May 24,1996

I must admit that I had more difficulty figuring out what day it is. Even now I don't know if I got it right. I have mixed emotions today and I have no one to talk to. I don't understand this disease really. It seems to me that I am functioning pretty well but Becky took me in for groceries yesterday- I don't think I said anything that wasn't rebuked in some way. Is this developing faster than I am ready to admit? I don't know what to expect really. I was surprised when Becky told Ora that I get mad at her at times. I don't think I have because I don't want to hurt her. But I have not been aware of getting upset with her. This morning I am very aware of one very important element missing from my life and that is my beloved husband.

During the years I've done a good job of being compatible with most everyone. Is that part of me disappearing or evaporating from me? How can I keep it? Will I be losing control of myself? I feel so alone right now. Will this feeling of helplessness just keep on worsening? Sometimes Becky or Deanna have made a remark of some sort that I find to be hurtful to me. Somehow these remarks seem to make me feel more useless each time. I'm trying so hard to do everything I can to keep functioning for as long as I can but I'm finding I must watch every word I say. Making the decision to quit driving may or may not have been the wisest because there are so few things I can do. It hurts to be treated as a child or dependent at this age. The Lord is really putting me to a test. Where I've always felt strength before, it is gone. I'm feeling useless as with no purpose or responsibility. I do what I can.

This was a period of time when neither my niece nor myself could say or do anything right. It seemed no matter how delicately we stated anything it was perceived as an attack at her. If we helped her prepare a meal, as was always the custom, she would sulk because we didn't think she could fix a meal anymore. If we talked on the telephone or to each other, even with her sitting with us, she felt we were talking about her. I believe she fought depression after learning she had Alzheimer's. This depression worsened as 1996 marched along. She would vehemently deny the possibility that she was depressed and become quieter and more sullen and refused to talk to us about what was going on with her. She tried so hard to be cheery and keep up a positive attitude.

Saturday, May 25, 1996

Truly, My Lord, you do work in mysterious ways your wonders to perform! Your love and care overwhelms me. Thank you! What a day this has been. Starting with the talk that Becky and I had yesterday afternoon. Today a very special Girl Scout staff member stopped to see me. What a blessing she was. Her father-in-law had had Alzheimer's and subsequently died with it. She put my mind to rest concerning some thoughts that had been troubling me.

I think it was such a blessing that she cared enough to come and visit me. It was a wonderful visit. I loved my Girl Scout work through the years and have never regretted the time spent with it. When Sharon called me the other day it was also very meaningful. The memories of the fellowship we shared while I was President of the Council have always been very special.

I bought a book in the Christian Book Store yesterday, purely a case of impulse buying, entitled 'The Healing Power of a Healthy Mind'. I am reading it. It relates how truth strengthens the immune system. Becky gave me a real good pep talk before she went home yesterday. When I started reading this new book, I could have sworn she might have written it. So I had a double dose of it, which is good.

May 26,1996

I had a disturbing experience this morning. I had waked up first at 4A.M. As usual, I started my morning prayers. However later, near 7, I think, my prayers were disturbing. I was using a book of prayers and thinking or meditating on them when I became aware of the fact that I could not remember a thing I had read. I pursued but it soon became frustrating because immediately after reading a prayer it was like someone or something instantly clutched any memory of the prayer from me. The more I tried to figure out my dilemma, the more frustrated I was becoming. Then I wondered was Satan deliberately taking the words from my heart and mind? I don't know but it still disturbs me! Can this be another stage of

Alzheimer's, that my memory is leaving me now or could it be Satan giving me a foretaste of what lies ahead? I couldn't stay in bed any longer. I was getting to frustrated. I came out to the living room where Jeanne had slept and told her about it. She put her arms around me and prayed for me- which seemed to help—

Friday, May 31,1996

I attended the funeral of a friend today. Since I have Alzheimer's now I feel very vulnerable in a funeral situation. My Precious Love, we would be celebrating our 49th wedding anniversary if you were still with me in person. But I am remembering and cherishing our very special day that we started our life's journey together. I do love you so very very much and I do look forward to our reunion in God's Kingdom. The only thing good about this Alzheimer's is I may be reunited with you sooner than I could have hoped for. Praise God!!

Tuesday- June 4,1996

My Trigeminal Neuralgia has returned. I'll have to see about acupuncture for it again. At least I had relief from it for the past 4-5 months.

June 28,1996

Since accepting the Alzheimer's diagnosis, I am gaining some new insights regarding my church. In the past, I have been told that different friends were disappointed because of church friends concerns when they were ill. "Why don't they care?" I thank you Lord, that you have drawn my personal attention to this same problem. I am understanding this better now that I am experiencing the same type of thing. There are bits of time that I wonder if Alzheimer's is like leprosy. Will people always be afraid of a person who is ill? In reality this is not contagious or harmful to others. I've always known that experience is the best teacher. But now the problem arises- Will I be able to express such a need to my pastor? I do not want to cause problems but I am now keenly aware of the telephone that hangs on the wall or sits on the desk or table that remains silent, day in and day out. Except for calls from my family or close friends. To hear the phone ring, to answer and be rewarded with the sincere expression such as, "How are you today?" would be so welcome. I am so grateful that I learned early in life to love people and show some concern for another persons' needs.

I confess my greatest fear of Alzheimer's is that it will cause me to lose my closeness to God.

Today the disturbing thoughts hovering around me regard my ability to remember. I do not want to lose my ability to pray and talk to God. It is different praying so much for my own concerns. Why do I feel so selfish praying for myself? I do believe my thoughts are being affected by the knowledge that my memory is fading. I do not want to lose the security of your loving care and possibly not knowing enough to abide in your love, Lord.

June 29,1996

I'm on medication now that is supposed to slow the progression of the disease. Yesterday morning I actually felt alive and vital again, for a real purpose. I enjoyed working around the house again and doing things with a purpose. Is the medication working? I do not handle my meds- so no mix up on my part. Remember the memory leaves the patient. That was the reason, most likely, for my excitement yesterday A.M. when I got the feeling of being alive and a real person- with a purpose ahead.

July 22,1996

Had a complete physical today. When the doctor asked me various questions, I was surprised that Becky interceded and gave several instances where it indicated some changes are occurring that I evidently had not noticed. I really can't find a way to describe my reaction to this insidious disease. I must admit after seeing the doctor I have wondered how much I have deteriorated. My days are spent here at home, generally by myself. I spend my days reading, doing embroidery or odd jobs and looking through things. I do not know what the rate of deterioration will be or how much time it will take. I'm probably not a good judge of the passage of time or its' effects on me. I don't feel that I have deteriorated overly much yet, but who am I to judge?

By this time Mom had been on Cognex for 10 months. The short-term memory lose is prevalent and paranoia seemed to be setting in strongly. Television was becoming increasingly disturbing to her. Nearly half the time she understood that the characters on TV were only acting, the other half of the time the characters were real and in her living room. Many times she would hurry to the TV to slap the cheek of a young person talking back to an adult. We started monitoring programs so she wouldn't get so upset.

Mom wouldn't remember when we told her about upcoming events. She would become upset that we weren't including her in everyday decisions, or asking her opinion on what she should do during the day. Deanna would take her Grandma with her when she would go home to Minneapolis for a weekend visit. Although Mom really enjoyed the opportunities to visit her other children in their homes, she did not like 'these sudden unplanned trips'. If she were told of an upcoming event to happen later in the week, time confused her and she would constantly be questioning why we didn't do whatever 'it' was. Her tongue would get pretty snippy if things didn't happen as she thought they should. Deanna and I decided that in to avoid these confrontations we would wait until the day of an event to discuss it with her. This helped reduce Mom's anxiousness considerably.

Leaving her for a few days didn't sit well with her, time was becoming incomprehensible. She would ask me how my trip had gone before I had taken it, and would become very angry with me for deserting her. She felt it was because I couldn't cope with her **"big disease"**.

Aug.1, 1996

I don't understand why, but as far as anyone else is concerned, I can do nothing right. Things had been looking up since seeing the neurologist. In fact, I'm working puzzles again. Why am I being constantly reminded that I do nothing right? It seems I am only a hindrance to a normal life, as I've known it. Am I feeling sorry for myself this morning? Very probably! I know Becky was busy with preparations to leave at 5a.m. this morning, but I called her about medicine because of the pain. I am not to take anything on my own. Because I can't be trusted! Yes, this Alzheimer's is a disease of destructive nature but can it be I just don't know anything anymore? Gracious Lord, I'm reaching out for help. I feel as though my natural personality is being stripped from me. Am I really a nothing? a useless individual that doesn't understand anything anymore. I can't be trusted to take medication, etc. After yesterday evening I feel as though I'm a totally useless personage who is only a nuisance to be stripped of my humanity. My feeling of personal worth is gone today. I need you my Lord, I do need you. Enable me to regain my self- esteem so I can cope with the surroundings. I have been stripped of all responsibility; it seems, because of my "Disease". I AM NOT A NOTHING. I AM YOUR CHILD, YOU ARE MY LORD, OUR LORD IN WHOM WE LIVE AND MOVE AND HAVE OUR BEING!

What a wonderful blessing I received this morning! Just when I thought Becky and Larry were long gone the door opened and in they walked. My hurt feelings of last night dissipated into the nothingness where it should have stayed. Bruised feelings were healed. Becky took the time to show me what meds I am taking and yes, it relieved me considerably! Will I remember the names? Maybe yes for some, maybe no for the new ones. Once again I felt some interest in my surroundings and meds because for the first time since the Alzheimer onset I was included, even though briefly.

One of the advantages I've gained in this experience is the extra time I've been privileged to spend with my daughters and granddaughter.

My husband, sons and I left for a two-week vacation on August first. Mom called me early that morning to find out what medication she could take while I was gone. I wondered if she thought she would be left unattended while I was gone. We stopped on our way out of town to reassure her that Deanna would be with her. My sisters had worked out a schedule to rotate care for her as well. But, while I was gone, there was too much activity around her. Because my siblings didn't deal with her on a daily basis, they had no idea how lost and confused she was by all the commotion. Deanna and I were very systematic with mother and she was comfortable with her usual ways. My sisters, taking turns bringing their families with them to care for mother, confused the security in her environment. Because she was very good at covering her inadequacies and confusion, they could not tell when she was confused or frustrated. I came home to a very angry mother. I read the writings mother did while I was away and I believe my sisters did too much for mother. They didn't know that they might better have served her by letting her do things at her own pace, figuring things out as she went along. That combined with the many different people coming and going, created quite a tangled web of confusion. When the primary caregiver must be away, it is best to have as few changes as possible in the dementia patients' environment.

Aug 3, 1996

My Precious Caretakers and Children and Grandchildren—

I realize that my illness has put each of you into a box, so to speak. It has done the same thing to me. It has not been easy for me either. I do believe that if you will think back over the past that my life has been made up of much more a sense of self worth than of pessimism and gloomy thoughts. My faith has been my strength. I do not want to hurt you in any way. It pains me to be a burden to anyone, it always has. I do believe the Lord has been working with me to help us bridge this gap in our relationship. I deeply regret my "complaints" to you. I will not make excuses but I do ask your forgiveness for my questioning. Yes, I have Alzheimer's but by the Lords help we cannot let it destroy our relationship. I am wondering if fear is the culprit. Yes, I do admit that I turned on a wrong burner on the stove once. I seriously question whether I put that towel in the oven. Never in my life have I used anything but a hot pad in the oven. But aside from that it is now past history, please do not keep reminding me of past instances as though I can never do anything right again. That by your words and attitudes I am merely a troublemaker. It pains me to be a burden to you or anyone. I pray that you will enable me to regain my sense of self worth and self-esteem so that we may get back on the track of a trusting relationship. Please enable me to be at least a little self-efficient again. I understand that you have a great fear regarding the medication, I accept that but by the same token I pray that you will not talk down to me as though I am a child incapable of any comprehension. Please help me to concentrate on and grow on the things I do right rather than judge my actions by one or two time events. With my Lords help I recognize that as of yet I am not incapable of understanding your viewpoints. Please talk to me as though I have some comprehension and ability to accept responsibility. Help me to regain and maintain the positive attitude of life and my faith that have been mine for these 74+ years. I must retain something of my self worth. I can't believe that our Lord will deliberately strip me of the personality that has always been what has made me. Please understand I am not criticizing any of you. I know my situation and it pains me considerably that I am a burden to any of you. This one thing I ask- Instead of talking down to me as a child who has no sense of responsibility and needs to be reminded of errors, talk to me as though I really do understand the situation I am in. When the time comes that you know I am totally without hope of continued improvement that has been evident, make the necessary arrangements for the nursing home.

The last thing I want is to be the burden I am led to believe that I am- and to become separated from the family we gave birth to have cherished all the years of our life together. Please do not take offense to what I have written before you. Give the words deep consideration of my feelings. Please bear in mind and remember that you have known me as a person who has been in control the majority of my life and I do believe I am still capable of understanding when I am talked to as an adult- not as being incapable of being trusted. Enable me to maintain my sense of self worth as long as possible. I do believe the Lord has been guiding my thoughts this morning and that He has enabled me to express my feelings to you for our joint understanding and to lay a firm basis to be able to avoid hurts and misunderstandings. With His grace and prayers we will succeed and remain "His family". I only ask that you remember I also have feelings- yet.

Can this be Saturday – Aug. 24, 1996?

I have been awake for hours. Seems like I have just been experiencing total disorientation through the night. The sun is up now- is making its' appearance- Thank you God. And I must get re-oriented. Why is disorientation such a problem? When I woke up during the night with the urge to go to the bathroom I was puzzled. Where am I? Then I remembered – I must be at Des Moines in Fletcher and Betty's home – But I couldn't remember where the bathroom was. After much reasoning, I came to the conclusion – no, this hallway I'm looking at is in my home in Willmar. Is it possible? Then, I must have slept for a while. Again when I woke, I couldn't remember who was sleeping where. Is someone in the bathroom? I couldn't get up and turn on the light to see- that would be interference or interruption. Well, that has never really been a habit of mine. In fact because I've always loved people and have made it a point to make them feel wanted and needed. But why can't I figure out where I am for sure? Lying here on my bed- it's getting lighter outside- morning is eventually coming- looking into the hallway from my bed- yes, I can see, this has to be my home. But I've been with Becky, I thought we had come to Fletcher's at Des Moines – but this isn't their home- Studying the hallway was confusing. Hallways are hallways- but the bathroom is on the left side- if the door is closed I'll have to wait. I can't just open the door and turn on the light – maybe someone else is in there!! So, I waited!! Until it was necessary to really get to the bathroom. Why, yes, as I went into the hallway, this was my house, my bathroom.

I must have gone back to sleep for a while. Someone was just up it seemed- but I don't see or hear anyone! Then, my thoughts turned to sister Betty. Why, I must be visiting Betty and Fletcher. No, I was alone here last night. But if I'm at Fletcher's? where is Fletcher? Again confusion- so I got out of bed and decided to write some of these thoughts down to help me deal with REALITY! –the quality that seems to be totally lacking from my life at this time – due to the Alzheimers', no doubt. This really is an insidious disease. Yes, I do have it- but usually I am not really aware of any real symptoms before- I've been able to do my work, cook, etc- No, it isn't quite the same in some ways- but it does seem I am coping pretty well. One fact I'm very aware of is- When I first saw the neurologist he told me I could be lucky- they had just found a new medicine that shows promise of helping Alzheimer patients. Yes, I have been encouraged by the news. So, Doc has been treating me with it. And it has seemed to be working. I feel more like myself. Other people tell me I don't seem to have this. But- after this night of confusion I must have it. Granted Sister Betty was on my mind, just why I'm not sure- but so is my baby brother, Fletcher- and he isn't here this morning- and hasn't been here for months and won't be. He is in his heavenly home with our parents, grandparents and ancestors. I must ask Becky- have I seen Betty since we left home? It seems I must not have- I don't know- she is never far from my thoughts because we are both widows!

Dear God, enable me to become oriented into the reality of my real situation. Thank you, I just remembered I spent the day with Becky yesterday, and a blessed one I'd say! I believe Kathy is coming later today. It will be good to see her. I don't know why and I can't waste time contemplating why Alzheimers' came to spend the remainder of my mortal life with me. I can only accept it – though I still thank you and praise you for some one discovering Cognex, this new medicine. I do pray that it will continue to be of help. If it be Thy Will, oh Lord. I hope for a longer life if I can be with my family in some way.

I do know that I am not the master of my fate, that I must cope with what comes my way. Most importantly, I also know that you, my Lord, will not give me more to handle than I can cope with. If there is some lesson or particular purpose in this for the benefit of my family, Precious Lord- I thank you- As of yet, I have found no benefits. I do know that I want You to be in control of *this disease- My life is in Your hands. May it be Thy Will that there is still something of vital importance for my children to learn from me? In all my way, my Lord, I will continue to trust in You and Your providence for my life. May I always keep fresh in my mind and heart daily that this is the day the Lord hath made, I will rejoice and be glad in it. Thank you Blessed Lord for listening and for walking with me on my journey. I thank you and praise you for the time I've been communing with you this morning. Thank you my Lord and Savior- Amen! The sun is shining- may it be a beautiful day for all of us!*

Sept. 1, 1996 - To my (our) children, Written following onset of Alzheimer's—

Good morning to each of you! Do you have any real understanding of how much each and every one of you and your families mean to me? I think you do but at this difficult time especially for each of you, but also for me.

I know you each love me in the fullest way. And I love each and every one of you to the utmost of my being. My most earnest desire is for a complete harmony between you. Is it possible that proximity to the farm is the reason for some misunderstanding?

No parents alive have shared a closer love than your Dad and I shared. We gave and shared that love with each of you. My mind is flashing back now to the countless special times we shared that happiness with our 6 children. I just can't think of any family I know that have shared more genuine happiness and love together.

In your baptisms we committed you into God's keeping, vowing to raise you in the way of the Lord. What, then, did the Lord require of us but to – do justice, to love mercy and to walk humbly with our Lord. As each of you was confirmed, you too accepted that vow. No one knows better than I and the Lord that we gave you the best we had to give by His grace. He was and is so very faithful always. Amen.

In retrospect the family times we shared, the trips, the horse shows, the tiredness each of us felt after getting ready for a horse show, the special pride we experienced as your Daddy sat on his horse performing to perfection.

I can never repay, in any way, the pride and gratitude I felt in each of you during the years when I was ill. You all came through with flying colors, taking on the responsibilities of your mother. God has and will continue to bless you through the difficult times that lie ahead of us.

Because I am older and have passed through the stage of losing Mother then Dad, I can be more realistic about my situation. I have attempted to keep an open mind and do continue to be very realistic in what lies ahead.

Yes, My loved ones, the road ahead is not and will not be easy for you for a while. It will take time to accept Gods' Will for my life and yours. Remember His promise. He will not give us more to bear than He is already giving us the ability and love to roll with the punches to accept the inevitable.

Yes, I accept the fact that each one has his or her own memories and you are all so even there. But, because Becky and Deanna are here, they are more involved with my care. Yes, care is so important. But, I do believe our family has always done a good job of sharing a very complete and full love that God will also use to carry us all through the Valley of the Shadow of Death.

Yes, Becky has lived the closest to us and this has been a special blessing, but never forget, for you who live at a distance, each of you have always been a special blessing also. I pray you will not begrudge or be proud of what each of you has been able to do in your own way. Most importantly, I trust each of you to the fullest extent. Your jobs, your responsibilities, family, school, etc. structures your time for everything you do. No one better than I know that you will be going through a very major time in your life. Always remember- as you handle adversity, you are also training your children and yourselves. Dearest Ones, each of you is so talented in many respects. Each of you is striving to do what is best for your Mother at this time. Yes, Becky has been privileged to live the closest to the home farm. The rest of you are doing your work at a distance farther away, where the Lord has placed you. One job is as important as the next one. Just be grateful for each other and I know you are. Aim to keep close family ties. I know from past experience that the hurdles ahead of you will be the hardest you will face. I can't soften the reality of how it will feel when I am gone. I ask you to find time amongst the tears to realize that Daddy and I are reunited, never again to be parted. From that beautiful vantage point we will eventually greet you to your Heavenly Home and "our big" reunion.

Moving into town????
Should do before winter sets in- BUT I'm secure here!!

Sept. 2, 1996

I AM <u>NOT</u> GOING TO MOVE TO MINNEAPOLIS!! It- the thought of it- absolutely frightens me beyond words.

Born and raised on the farm, the only time I was in a city (town) was that first year in Minnesota. I don't think I will be comfortable in any particular place away from this home your Dad built for us. It is my familiar home. Where I feel at home. Yes, I would like to spend a few days with my families in the cities- but I don't know really what my reaction to traffic and the noise of the city might be, if I were to move there into a home or? I don't know if I even begin to understand the full scope of this disease. Most importantly, I don't know what my capabilities are anymore, either. I guess the plain fact is that the "at sea" feeling I have at times is not comfortable at all. In fact, I do believe it will be best if I can stay in my home as long as possible. I guess I never have been really very adventuresome. I have decided that any "control" I've had in my life is coming to an end. Yes, I am comfortable as yet doing my own thing in my own home. Regardless of what decisions will need to be made I believe I will need the familiar setting to be able to accept the changes that have and are taking place within me.

Talking to Becky last night was a shock to me. Little did I realize how long I have had Alzheimer's? She is close enough for any need.

I intensely resent this invasion into my life at this time or any time. But this one thing I do know!! God will not give me more to handle than He will give me strength to cope with. I must rely on His promise for my peace of mind.

The program on the 'Lisa' show on Alzheimer's yesterday was a real eye-opener and a real shock regarding the effect of care by the family and the combative nature of the disease. This, too, is frightening!! I have asked God, "Why me?' but then I must follow that with "Well, why not?!" Can I really believe or know that I will be able to cope? I pray that I can. But only the Lord knows.

Sept. 15, 1996 –

A new, fresh week- Thank you Lord. I seek Thy help. The confusion and aloneness within me seems to grow. Why am I now helpless to regain my normally healthy perspective? What is this Alzheimer's doing to me? Yes, I appreciated Bill and Joan being here this weekend. (These are two long time friends who offered to spend the weekend with mom so that I could be gone for a business meeting in Northern Minnesota.) Does this mean that I must now pay to have someone come here to be with me because I can no longer be left alone? I'm still doing my cooking, housework, etc. but my family thinks I am not capable of being here alone. Do they think I am capable of harming myself? I gave up driving to put their minds at rest- but what more can I do? I've always felt that I learned the lesson of always being considerate of other people's feelings from Grandma, but I must be failing in that. Am I now becoming excess baggage? Aging is not easy- It is confusing and stifling- What is left for me to anticipate? I readily admit I miss my life mate tremendously and I am ready to rejoin him any time you call me home. Our family is self-sufficient and on there own and I am becoming a burden. How can I avoid this? Yes, Dear Lord, I do need your help. I am at a loss with this Alzheimer's. When I told Sam [minister] that I have it, I anticipated that he could help me to understand and accept it- His only remark was," I've seen this coming on you for a long time. I'm so glad I had the opportunity to work with you when you were sharp". Does this now mean I am a useless piece of junk? Precious Lord, I realize I'm having a "pity Betty party" this morning. I feel a need of being needed, some encouragement to keep on keeping on. Walk with me, my Lord, enabling me to keep a healthy perspective on the life I love. I know these thoughts are not healthy but I must get them out of my system. I must not harbor them in my mind and heart. I earnestly pray, my Lord that you will not let the Devil rob me of my sense of self worth. I need you always and forever. Oh, for my Grandmother's faith!

My Dearest Rebecca,

I am in bed but no sleep is possible- I feel so miserable. I don't really ever remember such words between us and oh, how they hurt. But please bear with me for a bit. I felt that I needed "a good cry"

75

*while you were doing chores- If only I had given in
then. But crying has never been easy for me- I've
always fought it- though I really don't know why. I
deeply regret the words tonight, even more I regret
having hurt you to this extent. I pray that you can and
that you will be able to forgive me for complaining as
you said. I admit I'm missing your Dad more and
more. Just why, I don't really know unless it has to do
with the Alzheimer's. I have to admit that it is very
difficult for me to face full force each morning that I
am facing my own mortality, that my time on God's
Earth and here at home is so measured and now I
realize I must make up to you some way because I have
been complaining about pain. I also admit that I don't
understand why you and Deanna give me absolutely no
slack but you expect me to go on as usual. My reaction
today could also possibly be due to Joan and Bill
telling me they were pleased to have such a good visit
and to find out I am still "Grandma Betty"-but
apparently I'm a stranger. But everyone doesn't see
this- perhaps they are wrong but it was encouraging to
me anyway. I really would love to call you right now
and apologize to you for my weaknesses but I'm sure
you are in bed and it would only upset you again.
These past months so many of my thoughts and prayers
have centered on prayers that during my last months
that I will have the privilege of seeing our children at
peace with each other. Then to really make matters
worse I crushed your spirit tonight, the very child I've
been the closest to. How can I seek your forgiveness?
I cannot cope with the distance between us. Please,
please forgive me and cut me a little slack. Please
remember that the certainty of my Home Going is a*

bridge that only I can cross. Yes, I can look forward to my Reunion with Dad and the other family members-but the other side of that coin is that before that reunion I must make myself strong enough to be able to tell each of my children Good-bye and my grandchildren. I have great difficulty even thinking about our separation and I know it won't get easier, but I also know as being your parent I must lead the way.

I appreciate so much the support you have given me, the miles you've driven to take me to your home so I won't be alone so many hours daily. But the way I've hurt you now is so hard to accept also. I do not understand exactly what this Alzheimer's is really doing to me other than being the gate to my entry into Heaven. When I say I remember this or that and someone says that's not right or that's not the way it was it has cut even deeper into what ever self esteem I may yet have. I know I am deteriorating but honestly it would help to have some encouragement also.

My death- rather my Home going as I prefer to think of it doesn't really scare me. What does bother me is the awful reality that the time is coming when I will be deteriorated and have to bid you all farewell-as I go to meet Our Lord, your Dad and other family who have gone before.

This is the most difficult walk I've had thus far in my 74 years. I feel I am not afraid to meet our Lord; in fact I virtually commit my life and soul to Him each day seeking His forgiveness. Yes, I do look forward to seeing our Lord in person and certainly to be reunited with your Dad and my Love. Please, remember that when my time comes that my last breath here will be immediately followed by my first breath in Heaven and Dad and I will be together. God knows I don't want to leave my family but He also knows I will have no choice. Please, please forgive me for my failures. I wish I could have been a better mother. I remember so well the times I was in the hospital in Worthington, and how much I hated to see you and Kathy being cheated out of your youth and fun activities because you girls became substitute parents or mothers to your siblings. I shall never forget the pride I felt in both of you. Please forgive me for being a complainer but I'm only human yet! I will make it a point to complain no more in spite of pain or whatever—

And now it is after 11 and I must be getting to sleep. I just wish I knew right now if you are able to forgive me for my failures. But I cannot open that horrible wound again tonight. We've shared such closeness through the years that I too, am deeply hurt because I have wounded you- my right hand- I promise to regain my positive attitude but please cut me a little slack because of the disease that I can do nothing about but to accept it and roll with the punches.

You may share this with Deanna if you like. I haven't been able to talk to her of my impending "Home Going" yet. Always remember- we well be separated for a time but to look forward to the Great Reunion of the far future ahead.

My deepest love to you and yours- Good night and God's Blessings

My precious girls – Please remember this is also hard on me – whether I complain or be cheerful. It is just not easy!!

This morning I am particularly aware of the countless times I've bored both of you with questions, repeatedly the same. But I am keenly aware of the feeling of having no control over any memory, short term or long term. I am realizing more each day that I have no control over anything. I am becoming a piece of junk to be cast aside out of harms way. This behavior is so foreign to my lifetime personality. I confess it, the Alzheimer's, is now my master and controller. I wish I could have some quality of life long enough to mend fences but even that seems to be out of my reach. I do believe I can cope with the loss of your love but I will try to make things as easy as I can. Between the Alzheimer's and Satan I am no longer the me I have been. I am so grateful Dad has been spared the pain of seeing his "angel of the morning" becoming a nothing, a useless piece of junk. I shall concentrate on the new person I will become when my- our- God calls me Home. I will try even harder to control the words that come out of my mouth. Please try to remember my deep, deep love and appreciation for you both and for being willing to be my caretakers- and that this too will pass and you can return to some normalcy in your lives. I could not foresee what a huge task you girls were undertaking.

My dear Deanna- you are so capable but it hurts me dreadfully to be taking your youth and freedom from you. I did not ask for this disease and I feel so helpless and useless. Yet I'm beginning to feel that I simply do not know who I am anymore.

Gracious Lord- I commit my life into Your hands. Thank you for helping me to walk this narrow lonely path that lies ahead. Please surround my caretakers with Thy everlasting Love and protect them from what I am becoming—

Gracious and merciful Lord, please enable me to find the person I was once so bad memories can be erased forever.

Wednesday noon, Sept. 25, 1996

Pastor Sam has just left following a Pastoral call. I find that it was helpful in many respects. Time will tell! I simply must remember that my short-term memory is definitely going. I am so glad he verified for me that he had called on me earlier this summer. I am sorry that I told Becky I would surely have remembered the visit, but I did not!! Again I must apologize to Becky. I am very pleased that she has taken the time many times to explain to me there are things I am forgetting. I know there are changes taking place I have not been aware of. I'm so glad Becky has been following the reality of this devastating illness that has taken possession of my body in spite of me. Sam has also convinced me that I must deal with differences in family attitudes and that decisions must be made relatively soon. Yes, this is a disease that robs me of being me. I must deal with things now. I must accept the fact that the short-term memory just does not exist anymore. Yes, I must continue to face the very real reality of the situation. With this in mind I must in some way – how, I don't know –convince my family that I cannot move to Minneapolis. It simply petrifies me to death. Yes, I would love to know my grandchildren better and well enough for them to remember something good about me. I could maybe go in for a day or so but I just can't live in there indefinitely. This is my home. The home Birk built for us and so filled with his love and the beautiful memories we shared here. My earnest desire is to remain here where I still feel that precious love.

My Precious husband, 9-27-96

I have clothes in the washing machine and a busy day looms ahead. Today is a meeting with our children. What to do about Mom?

I am afraid I will put a monkey wrench in any plans of moving to Minneapolis. This is so frightening to me because I have never lived in the cities. A visit is one thing but to live there petrifies me. The complicating factor is the Alzheimer's disease! My Dearest Husband I have to say that I am glad you are not here to see the subtle changes in me. I'm still able to be safe and secure here. I truly want to stay here as long as possible. You built this home for us and at this time it has become my security blanket. I feel safe here. This is indeed a new experience for me and I confess it is frightening at times. I certainly appreciate Becky's and Deanna's care and concern.

One of the typical problems with this disease is wandering. I haven't walked anywhere but to the mailbox occasionally. That is one of my major fears about strange surroundings. So far, locked firmly in my mind and heart is the security I feel here in our home. I do seem to feel your warmth and the security it gives me and I feel content. It's when I get into strange surroundings that I feel disconnected. My dearest Love, I do so hate to be a burden to our blessed family. The fact remains that I am noticing changes in me and it bothers me because I feel that the time is coming when I will feel even more out to sea. I still feel safe and secure here and I take satisfaction and safety that Becky is as close as the telephone if I had a real need. I do believe I have handled things very well so far. Becky and Deanna do not cut me much slack for error and I feel security in that. My heart aches for our children who are not as involved in this. I know they are hurt because they live farther away and they are not able to see what is happening, consequently there will be less understanding from them. No one knows better than I that this is a horrible disease. Will I end up in an Alzheimer's unit? There is one in town. Sam suggested I get my name on the waiting list, just in case it would be necessary. Because the time will come when I need assistance and in depth care.

I am still doing my own work. I haven't made rolls for a while but the joy I had in making them is no longer here. You see I dearly cherished seeing you on bread baking day when you would come in from doing chores and would rather impatiently wait until the first hot rolls came out of the oven

The family joined at mothers home this weekend to discuss with her the options she had regarding different living arrangements. They had investigated various facilities in the Twin Cities area and some nearer to mother's home. Mom stated to them that she would like to stay in her home as long as she felt comfortable. She shared with them her fears in leaving her home but did agree, "that when the time comes that I no longer know where I am," she would go to a different place. This did not sit well with my brother and sister. They felt she would be better cared for in a facility and that her love of people and socializing would help her to adjust. If she relocated to the Twin Cities area, it would allow more frequent visits from more of her children and grandchildren. The family would be able to take turns visiting, relieving the responsibility from just one person. I felt strongly that it would be best for mom to stay in the familiar environment and routine of her home for as long as possible. I feared that a move to unfamiliar territory would hamper her mental well-being, that it would increase the confusion and anxiety she was already experiencing, and possibly shorten the time her memories would be shared with us. Mother felt the tension. Disliked the fighting among us, and was upset that they would not listen to her. We took the remainder of the meeting to my house to discuss her future. It greatly offended mom that a so-called "babysitter" had to stay with her when we departed. On mother's behalf, Deanna and I presented our views from the experiences we shared of caring for her on a daily basis. The others rebutted with the knowledge taken from what they had read about Alzheimer's disease. In the end, Mother was allowed to stay in her home, but only if Deanna and I followed a few new rules imposed on us by the others.

9-27-96

Gracious and Precious Lord of my life. I deeply regret that I am inflicted with this insidious disease called Alzheimers'. It seems to be obvious that I am driving my family away from me. None of us can really understand this devastating disease. The last thing that I want to happen is to be is totally alone and away from these children that Birk and I gave life to. Thank you, Precious Lord, for all you've done for me. I need your help so very much. Right now I feel totally devastated and so alone. It is becoming quite obvious that I am failing in being the parent that I've been in the past. Please forgive me Gracious Lord and help me through this most painful period. It appears that I have failed my family and hurt them so deeply. Yes this does devastate me. I've never had this before and I do know that I do not like what it has done and is doing to my family and me. Help me, Dear Lord, to find or understand what I must do to save my family. This is so devastating for each of us. Dad and I were always so proud of our precious family. Does this mean that I am single handedly forcing the break up of the beautiful family we had so lovingly created? How can I regain the love of my family? My wisdom has failed me and I deeply regret words spoken earlier. I pray that you will enable me to regain my family. Remove all sense of self-pity from my soul and heart. I pray you will enable me to be the parent you intended me to be.

Christmas Season 1996

This year of 1996 has been a totally new experience for me. It is 2 years ago that I was diagnosed with Alzheimer's. I tried to accept the verdict as best I could but it is not easy. This is like a thief in the night that takes my memory away before it can become a part of me.

November and December was a very mild and enjoyable winter, but the snow and wind that accompanied January nearly buried us alive. No matter how warm it was in the house, mother would complain she was cold and she burned a lot of calories turning up the thermostats throughout the house. We sneaked quietly behind her turning them back down. Then we discovered that the curtains were closed mom couldn't see the snow and her complaining diminished.

Early in January our area was hit with one storm after another. I did not want to be snowbound at mothers with a diabetic niece and mom with no way to get out in case of emergency. I moved them to my house for a couple of weeks. During this time, my husband and I realized it would not be a wise to have mother move in with us when her disease progressed to needing constant care. She was familiar with our home, but it became apparent that the activities of my family were too much for her to handle.

Still at Becky's home. I have been gone from home now for 2 weeks probably 3. Rode out to the farm with Becky today. Much, much snow. We couldn't get in the driveway. I visited with the neighbors while Becky was at my house. It seems so strange to be so close and yet so far from my home base! Sometimes I wonder if and when things will return to some normalcy! This winter is a winter like we had years and years ago!! What a contrast the automatic heat is to the hand-fired furnace of so many years ago. My furnace is fuel oil. Becky said it is running fine. But in this severe cold how long will the fuel last? I am concerned about the uncertainty of not knowing just what is going on there in my absence. Because I don't drive anymore I can only trust that it is all ok. Deanna is going into town. She said Chris is here with me. Why is it I can't be alone anymore? Somehow I feel I gave up a lot when I decided to quit driving because of the Alzheimer's. I seem to be losing my self-esteem because I'm not trusted to make any decisions for myself. I don't like these feelings but I don't know what I can do about them. I don't like to accept the apparent fact that I am incompetent. What can I do to change this impression? I'm very grateful that my family is concerned for my welfare and I would like to be involved in the so-called family discussions!!

Jan. 26, 1997

Still at Becky's. How I long to return to my own home. Yes, I realize it is easier for Becky, but is it for me? I honestly don't know!! I am becoming convinced that life is easier for me if I can stay busy doing something constructive. I know that my knee and hip are especially painful but I don't know that there is much to be done about it [the pain] for a short period of time. Health-wise, I think I do pretty well, but it is difficult at times. This has been a most unusual winter. I just wish I wouldn't feel out of place or disjointed so to speak. How much is this Alzheimer's' affecting me? I know the ultimate outcome of this disease. Now I am wondering when and also hoping for my ultimate release.

Feb. 17, 1997 Monday A.M.

Thank you Lord for this, another day. I am in my own home. What I don't know is who else might still be here and still sleeping. Becky brought me home last night. Deanna is here but apparently is not up yet. Becky doesn't want me to be alone too much and honestly I don't know exactly what to think about it. There are times I try to figure out a way to understand this humiliating disease but just can't find a proper word. One minute I'm part of a loving family then the house empties out and I'm alone, at least for a while and I begin to get uneasy. Why? I don't know, but I presume it is the Alzheimer part of the picture. I try not to second-guess my situation but I still have questions. There just may be no answers for my quandary. One disappointment I have is that I'm developing shakiness. This bothers me because I've often solved a problem by writing my thoughts down. I find it to be a great help for me. Shakiness limits this aid for me. I do pray I will not alienate my family through this rough time. It is hard on everyone not just me!!!

In August 1995, my niece, Deanna, moved 100 miles away from her family to live with her grandmother. At the time, mother didn't need a full time caregiver; she needed her because she of loneliness and her need to be needed. Deanna filled those needs for her.   Deanna would remain with mother until she was married in September of 1998. It took great courage for this 17-year-old to move so far from her family, and to change schools for her senior year of high school. There was apprehension by the rest of our family regarding this decision; Deanna is diabetic and they feared the move and the stress of living with grandma would make it hard to control her diabetes. It was Deanna's choice. She chose to live with and care for her grandmother out of love and respect she felt for her. During her stay she did not have the problems her family worried about.

Deanna's move to moms was very helpful to me. It allowed me to continue working outside the home and to care for my family without having to constantly worry about mother.   The two of us had a pretty effective system that allowed mom to have her freedoms as well as us. We didn't want her to become dependent on either one of us until it was obvious that she would no longer be able to do things for herself.

As time passed and mother's condition worsened, I needed to be with her while Deanna was at work or in school.   We were able to leave her alone for short periods of time between our shift changes and for a while I was still able to go home after mother had retired for the evening. If left alone too long, she would become confused with the amount of time she had been alone and feel that she had been neglected. She would get lonely and angry with us for never coming to see her. Deanna and I did not worry, at this time, that mom would wander off or endanger herself in any way.

Soon, I was no longer working outside of my home and my husband and sons could fend for themselves; I was able to be with mother whenever Deanna was away. Now spending 14 or more hours per shift with mom, my brothers and sisters became worried about my health. They had learned that caregivers often become ill or worn out and unable to adequately care for the patient. They felt I couldn't make rational decisions regarding Mom's care and so another family meeting was scheduled. This time we met with a mediator from the Minneapolis Alzheimer organization. Deanna and all six children were present. Nothing was settled there but we learned that we needed counseling to resolve our differences. We continued the meeting at my sister's home. I remember, so vividly, sitting while my family lambasted me with what they wanted for mom, and to tell Deanna and I that we didn't know what we were doing. I could understand how they felt, we all loved our mother and we only wanted what was best for her. Why couldn't they understand where I was coming from? We had just agreed that it was O.K. to disagree, but I was not allowed to disagree with them. One brother felt that it would be best to care for mother in her home and that if I was willing to continue caring for her, they should be supportive and help me with my decision. It was also decided that if Deanna and I wanted to continue to care for mother, we would have to keep a daily journal and hire respite care. I left that meeting with chest pains. I could not believe that this loving, tender family, that I thought I understood, was capable of so much bitterness and hate. Exactly what mother never wanted, the tension and anger among us, exploded that day. There was now a breech in our relationships. It hurt deeply to loose the closeness we had always had in the past.

At this point, I believe it is necessary to discuss the extreme pressure(s) on each person involved in an Alzheimer patients care. We are human beings, with strong emotions, individual view's, bias's, knowledge and lack of knowledge. Fears for the unknowns, money issues, different geological locations, etc. are only a few of the issues that will cause friction between family members and loved ones involved in caring for a dementia patient. It is my sincere hope that no one will go through difficult times during decision making processes...but the truth be told, no matter who you are, if there are others involved in those decision, there is a very, very good chance that there will be disagreements. Feelings are vulnerable along this path.

For me, I had never anticipated the degree of difference in our beliefs regarding Mother's care. It was an extremely difficult time for all of us; I was surprised, angry, hurt, shocked, scared, and felt victimized and ignored. I knew my capabilities and my limits...I was prepared and wanting to continue this journey with Mother in her home. My brothers and sisters were discussing what they felt was best for mother and me. They wanted to relocate her and put her into an institution; that would also relieve my commitment. I didn't feel their trust in my choices nor did I feel they gave high regard to Mother's abilities, emotions and wishes. Whether or not this was true, and whether or not this was anyone's intent, is really beside the point. These struggles are a reality in caring for a loved one and in deciding their future. No one person is necessarily right or wrong…but it will feel right or wrong (in the moment) and it is extremely important to prepare for these difficult times. They will show up…at different times, in different ways, for different people and for many different reasons!

I spent my days with mother and I knew we were capable of journaling, but I did not call in respite care until just before Deanna was married.

Following this meeting I wrote my feelings to my family:

I question if I am right or wrong. Am I doing what is best for mom or am I hurting her? When four of my siblings think I am being a martyr or following selfish ideas I really wonder if I am wrong in caring for our mother.

All week the Bible verse 'What does the Lord require of you but to do justice, love kindness and walk humbly with Him', has played near none stop in my head. The Bible also tells us to care for the widows and our families.

Mom asked Deanna and I to help her stay independent as long as possible. She has told all of us she wants to stay in her own home until she doesn't know she is leaving there. I do not wish to create a riff in this family. I only wish to care for our mother as I have been charged to. What are we doing that is so wrong? We are helping her to maintain her dignity, her sense of belonging, and her independence. She still feels useful and vital in her home and community.

Yes, there are things she cannot do anymore, things that were once second nature to her. It tears my heart to see these things but what tears even worse is watching her try to cover it. At times she is as a forlorn bewildered puppy. She is so afraid of letting anyone see her this way and so we carefully guide her and not let on that we see the bewilderment. And the again, sometimes she knows we know so we talk about it. It is frightening to her. She has always been the one others turn to for help and answers. Now she is afraid to let others see her 'like this'-a weakling with no brain [her words]. She doesn't want anyone feeling obligated to her. She doesn't want to be a burden to anyone. So when it is suggested to her that she live elsewhere she thinks that would be good because she wouldn't be a burden to Becky and Deanna. But she's not a burden. We choose to care for her. Being mom's caregiver is not always easy. It is sometimes frustrating and always – always- watching her stumble and grasp for her wholeness is painful. But never do I feel I was pushed into this by anyone. Priorities and choice these are what rules each of us. I choose to be mom's caregiver. I choose to make her top priority in my life. I am very honored to have a husband that supports me in my choice.

Alzheimer's is a weird disease. It cannot be put down in solid 'stages'. It has no definite guidelines for when this happens or that happens. It can be and always will end cruelly. No case is the same. No two days are the same for mom. She definitely has what's called 'sun downing' around 4:00p.m. And she basically needs to be in bed by 8-8:30p.m. She doesn't function well when she is tired. No one does. One minute she can be totally confused and the next she's not. Some days are good, some days are good and bad, and then some days are just plain BAD. Our mother still has her ability to reason. She may not remember everything all the time. She may not remember on her own to take her meds but she is not in danger to herself or anyone else and she is not in danger of wandering off. She needs to be able to move about in her home with no one watching her so that she can fumble in her own time privately to find her bearings. Right now she needs her private time to deal with what she knows is happening to her.

We need emotional support. We need the freedom of unloading the bad and difficult things on our family so that we can keep on accepting the changes happening to our mother. We shouldn't be afraid that if we say something you can't deal with you won't immediately say she needs to be moved.

Sit with her, laugh with her, cry with her. Listen to the memories that just popped into her head. Take the time to live in her world, to feel her joys and her disappointments. Allow her to be who she is at that moment. Put yourselves in her shoes. She isn't a mindless person you can't talk to or reason with. No, she isn't totally capable of making her own decisions but she is still a viable person with her own thoughts and feelings. She is not the same as she was a year ago. That doesn't mean she needs a different environment. Moving her out of her home would be a mistake. We will ALL lose.

At this point I need to add that the only stress I ever felt while caring for mother was the stress induced by my siblings. I couldn't understand how not-too-long-ago I was capable of making wise decisions.

Not-too-long-ago they all had trusted me to watch out for both our parents. It hurt a great deal to loose their support but I could not give up on our mom by moving her out of her home to a facility. We had all been taught that love would win out. I had to believe that it would.

Mom and I kept a pretty active social schedule. She had friends who would invite her to their homes or visit Mother in her home when Deanna and I needed to be away. If I had a lot to do at my house Deanna would bring her in to me on her way to school or work. Mom would help me with my projects in the garden and with my sewing business. She loved to do handwork, sewing on buttons, snaps, and hemming garments. As time passed it was easy to see her deterioration in her sewing capabilities. I allowed her to do handwork long after she wasn't able to. It made her feel useful and gave her something to do. I could always redo her work after she went to bed.

Keeping a daily log, we were able see that the moon, weather, and pain made definite differences in her mood. Her disposition varied with the weather. A cloudy overcast morning meant she was usually very negative. As the day brightened or the sun came out, her disposition would also brighten. Her confusion would wax and wane with the moon. About a week before a full moon, she would begin getting more agitated and disconnected. The days following she would improve. The same thing would happen around a new moon but would be for a shorter length of time.

Her confusion and nasty attitude were also aggravated by the level of pain she was experiencing.

On April 28,1997, I took mom for an interview with Elderly Day Services. Mom's dearest friend, Thelma, enjoyed the program and felt mom would benefit from it. EDS operated out of one of the local nursing homes. She was very nervous and apprehensive during the interview. They signed her up for the same days as Thelma. I had never seen my mother so nervous or frightened of anything. While I drove her home she questioned what she would do without her home. Who would take care of her house? She was afraid I would leave her at the nursing home and not come back. I thought she had understood that this would be an outing for the day, not moving into the nursing home. The next day was to be her first day. It was April 29, 1997... I was helping her get ready and would drive her to EDS. She dragged her feet getting ready and came up with numerous excuses why she shouldn't go. She was very uneasy when we arrived. I reassured her I would be back at 3:00, and took my leave. Like a mother sending her child to their first day of school, I worried all day about how she was coping. 3:00 came and I was right there to pick her up as promised, only to find her in no hurry to leave. She was busy laughing and talking to new friends. It had been a great day and she was glad she had decided to go. For the most part Mom attended EDS three days a week until she passed away. The program was very good for her and was important respite time for me.

Rebecca Clark

June 2, 1997

I feel quite naked and vulnerable like a fish out of water! Where do I belong? There is no time frame for anything. I am not comfortable being like a fish out of water.

Through summer and fall Mom helped me with my garden and putting my harvest up for winter. I remember, one afternoon her snapping green beans to prepare them for freezing. Using a small paring knife she would diligently cut the ends off the beans. This task went smoothly for a while; then I noticed she had stopped and was seemingly bewildered. While doing something else, I watched out the corner of my eye to see what was happening. She started cutting one bean on both ends, then, appeared to be at a loss at what to do next. A moment later she would cut the bean pieces that she had just cut again. She would stop and repeat the same process. The frustration was beginning to show. I picked up another paring knife, sat in front of her and she watched as I cut the ends off my bean, then cut it between its seeds and put the freshly cut pieces in the pan. I picked up another bean and repeated the process. We talked, while I cut, about everything except how to cut the beans. I cut quite a few beans before she finally started cutting the beans with me. It seemed that even this simple repetitious task had become a difficult chore. We had some pretty tiny pieces of string beans with our meals that winter!

Aug. 27, 1997—

Just got home from Becky's. Helped her with canning pears this morning. My back has been especially painful this day. At this point I am beginning to wonder if I'm up to a trip to Colorado. Yet, I know I want so very much to go to Danny's and Elizabeth's wedding. Something must improve for me. Yes, I know I am aging and things are more difficult, but I've never really been a quitter so I must fight on! I've enjoyed helping Becky with the fruit canning. But I guess I won't be trying to do any for myself. Maybe after I get back from Col. Time will tell. I find it very difficult to accept the reality of the fact that all the work from the past- gardening, canning, bread making, Girl Scouts, 4-H, etc. are from the past. I do not regret the things I was able to do in the past. They were enjoyable at the time and a very rewarding feeling to have garden produce and fruit stored in the basement for the winter months. I must accept the fact that I am no longer young and able to do as much as I used to do. All things considered I do believe I've served my loved one to the best of my ability. Will I ever hear my Lord say, "Well done Thou good and faithful servant"?

Mom did go to Colorado for my sons wedding. She and Deanna flew out for the weekend and we had plenty of family to help look after her. The wedding day was long and tiring for her but she had so much fun! One very special event for her was dancing with my son, Dan, after the ceremony. She always said she couldn't dance, a fact that was collaborated by Dad when he was alive. The day of the wedding she was a natural! While the bride and groom danced the first dance, guests blew bubbles at them. After blowing some on her grandson and his new wife, Mom snuck around the crowd to blow bubbles at Deanna and her fiancé, Ryan. She had forgotten that they had set their wedding date for the next September and wanted to give them a little push in the marriage direction.

October 13,1997 I wrote in our daily log: I don't write in here everyday anymore as mom's condition has been deteriorating gradually since April. Her good days now are simply days that she doesn't complain about one thing or another or that she can simply remember what she just heard for 5 minutes. These days are infrequent now. There still is a definite decline in mental abilities around a new or full moon.

I cannot detect any short-term memory 90% of the time now. Although she will at any given time, a few days to a week after an event, recall the event as though it was either many years ago or a few minutes earlier. Unless you know what she is relating to she can still sound sensible and with it. It is still easy for her to converse with others.

Deanna related to me that mom hadn't taken a shower for at least a week. When I instructed mom to take her shower and let the warm water sooth her aching back she had many excuses not to. I thought maybe she couldn't remember how to operate the shower. I was wrong. *"Dick hasn't started the furnace yet."* What does that have to do with taking a shower was my reply. *"There isn't any hot water!"* She thought the hot water furnace is what gave her hot water for her shower. She became upset and pouted when I explained the furnace and hot water heater were 2 separate things. *"When did we change that?!"*

She cried looking at the pictures of Dan and Elizabeth's wedding. I asked what was wrong. *"You told me I was there, I just wish I could remember."* Mom's friend Alice had called me about the possibility of mom hosting their Bible Study in a couple weeks. I told her yes she could with my help. Alice told me all about the how beautiful the wedding sounded and how pleased she was for me that all went well. I questioned how she knew that and she replied mom had told her all about it the Sunday she and Deanna had returned from Colorado.

Mom is always talking to herself now. She reads everything out loud to me even when I told her I had just read it. The odd part is that she reads the newspaper 3-4 times a day and each time she reads to me the same article she read to me the time before. It is interesting that from the first reading at noon to the last reading before bed it is always the same article that catches her attention.

She has become nosey. We catch her going through our things both at her house and mine. She gets pretty indignant that it is <u>her</u> stuff not someone else's when called on it. I have to watch her closely in stores now as she is inclined to pick up and pocket things.

I am concerned about her eating habits. She continues to loose weight. She loves junk food. There's never a problem getting her to eat ice cream or chips. These foods can be used to bribe her to eat her meals but it doesn't work very often. She remembers eating her morning cereal only if she sees a dirty bowl in the sink. Some mornings I will quietly wash her bowl and spoon and put them back in the cupboard before I ask her if she has had her breakfast. Always she will check the sink and seeing no cereal bowl will fix another breakfast.

She continues to have loose stool and it doesn't seem to matter what she eats. She drinks plenty of water. Tests at the hospital this summer showed nothing physically causing the problems. This is a side effect of the Cognex. In view of the fact that she has been failing mentally since April and the stomach problems continue, I wonder if we should keep her on the Cognex. Perhaps she should be put on the new Alzheimer medicine. What will happen if we take her off the Cognex? Is it doing her any good? Are we wasting her money?

Nov. 11,1997

Mother returned this afternoon from Minneapolis after 4 days with her children and acupuncture treatments. I am with her from 9:45p.m. - 12:00a.m. She is very shaky, talking with clinched teeth barely opening her jaws. She is very frail looking and acting. Her last meal was at noon. I gave her some chicken soup. She says she doesn't feel good and is full. She has no recollection of where she had been but knew she had been gone. She couldn't remember how she got home. Very confused. Went to bed at 11:30p.m. Stomach felt better but still very shaky.

Nov.15, 1997

Full moon. Totally not here today! When I arrived early this morning Deanna reported that grandma was acting funny, acting as though she didn't see her and was picking at the air. I watched her move slowly around the house opening drawers carefully putting nothing in and taking something out then moving to the next imagined task, all the while talking to someone I could not see. When I spoke to her she would look beyond me, sometimes thru me, and not see me. There was a different world in her eyes. One I could only guess at trying to fit into. I cried inside as I watched this complete stranger that just yesterday had been my mom. I had to dress her as she could not come into my world enough to do so herself or even help me help her. She finally quit wandering and sat on the sofa. She visited with her friend while she played with her shoes tying and untying the laces until they were full of knots. Most of her talk was gibberish but I could deduce she was talking to her grandmother and other relatives from her distant past. Presently she looked at me. Very clearly she said *"I don't think that is a very good place for that picture"*, as she pointed to the floor in front of her. I walked over, looked where she pointed and said, "You're right. That's not a good place for it". As I bent down to carefully pick up her imagined picture I commented on what a beautiful picture Nellie had painted. *"She is very talented."* Carefully I hung and straightened it on the wall then stepped back to admire it with her. *"That's much better,"* she said and went back to talking to her imagined friend and picking imaginary things out of the air. [That day I learned again two important things; the importance of validating her words and actions and the importance of living in her world where ever it would be.] Mother spent most of her day in this 'other' world. I spent mine crying and mourning the loss of yet another part of my mother. I had worked in nursing homes and had seen many old folk going through these same actions. Was this what we had to look forward to? Was her mind going to just suddenly leave her like this and never return? Watching her tore me apart emotionally. She started coming out of that world about mid afternoon. As the evening went by she returned to her normal self. Many times I had driven home after leaving mom and Deanna and cried over the changes I had seen that day. This night I had to pull off the road. An ocean of tears blocked my sight. I decided that if I was going to be able to continue caring for mom, watching her slowly, yet quickly, deteriorate before my eyes daily, I had to detach myself emotionally from her. I could no longer look at her as my mother. I would have to pretend she was just someone I was caring for. It was not easy to detach myself like that. I started by allowing myself to be her daughter the first hour I was with her each day and gradually shortened it to not allowing myself those feelings at all unless I was away from her for a few days. I don't believe I could have managed the duration of her disease had I not done that.

Luckily we never experienced another day like this one.

By the end of 1997 we were not able to leave mom alone at all. The concept of time was just to difficult for her to grasp and the tongue lashings we could get for 'neglecting' her just weren't worth it.

1998

We did not write much in our journal during 1998. Mom's trips to Minneapolis with Deanna gradually became burdensome on everyone there. She did not like the long drives and would get angry that Deanna wouldn't take her home. She had to be watched carefully so she wouldn't open the car door while they were driving. The different floor plans of her children's homes would create a panic in her that would keep her confused. I would get calls from the family. They would ask how to get Mom redirected, or how to squelch her anger, or various "how to's". Not having been around her as much as Deanna and I, they did not know how to handle – what was to them – her odd behaviors.

Jeanne's home was laid out much like Moms home, so she could function there best. The only problem there was the noise of all the grandchildren. As her confusion grew, her patience with the little ones decreased. It was hard for the youngest ones to understand what was happening to their grandma. My sisters and brothers had very busy lives so it was difficult for them to find time to travel to Mothers home. When Deanna took grandma home with her, it was good for all of us. Unfortunately, as the year wore on, Deanna's rejuvenation from a weekend visit was undone by the time she drove her grandma the three hours back home.

In August, my husband and I had to be away for two weeks. We asked a couple that Mom knew well and felt comfortable with stay with her and Deanna. When we returned, Deanna moved back to her parents' home to finish preparing for her wedding in September. I moved to mothers. My husband supported me in my endeavor to continue caring for mom even though it meant leaving him to deal with his teenage son alone. Two friends came on board to help with moms care and provide respite care for me. The three of us set up a rotating schedule that actually allowed me more time away from mom than I had been having.

Mom wrote infrequently about what was happening with her. She would try, but her hands were so shaky she wasn't able to write much. Most of her writings were in letters to loved ones and friends, but didn't make much sense. Most of them never got sent. Actually, most of them weren't found until I went through her books, notebooks and belongings after her death. She would write in anything and on everything. In one book I found written with shaky handwriting; *'Is mother still alive?'* In another is written; *'I pray something good will come out of my experience with Alzheimer Disease for my family and others if it be Thy Holy Will.'* She had started underlining what she was reading so that she would know what she had already read. In her prayer book she highlighted prayers – keep me from feeling sorry for myself – give me patience to await Your deliverance. If it should be

Your will that I linger on my sickbed, grant me the confidence that You do all things well. When Your will is accomplished in me, deliver me from this cross that You have laid on me.

On January 26,1999 I again wrote my thoughts in our journal.

I feel a need to express our experiences of 1998.

Because the side effects of the Cognex were affecting mom and her mental decline continued gradually the Neurologist began the 6-week withdrawal from that drug. If we saw a difference in her attitude or mental decline then he would put her on Aricept. Unfortunately Deanna and I could detect no difference. We didn't feel it would do any good. Should we spend the money on this new drug? I wrestled with the thoughts that perhaps I would hasten her dementia if I didn't start the new drug. Talking with the doctor helped me to decide to try it for two months. If it didn't help the dementia it would at least help curb the anger that had been growing in mom as she came off the Cognex. Paranoia became obvious in mom. Everyone was against her, plotting to be rid of her. Mother had struck at Deanna several times and was very lippy with her. She did not behave this way with me. It was at this time that she began confusing me with her mother. When she would get cranky with me I would tell her that if she was going to act like that she could go to her room until her attitude changed. If she obeyed then I knew I was 'mother', if not then she would reprimand me for speaking to her as if she were a child. After the two month trial the Aricept did not create any differences so it was stopped. Her rate of decline stayed gradual until August. Perhaps it was because of my short absence and all the hubbub of Deanna's moving out and my moving in. Changes in her routine caused irritability. We did notice that she did not rebound back to her usual self after the full moon episodes. Each full moon episode seems to have taken more of her mind. She has not recovered much from the full moon of December and now we are headed into the second full moon of January. What will this one take away from her?

Around July we noticed she had difficulty recalling her past. This has now become nearly completely garbled. I was kept challenged through summer and fall by trying to figure out who I was at any given time in her mind. Being her mother or myself wasn't too difficult but she added more persons for me to be. The most difficult was when I was her sister. Mother didn't have a sister. When I would try to fit in my Aunt who she called "Sis" that wasn't right. Maybe she was another Aunt that mom had traveled with before they had both gotten married. Nope, that didn't work either. Who 'sister' could possibly be, was beyond me. Occasionally, my not fitting the character in her mind did not faze her. Usually if I couldn't connect fast enough she would get mad and throw a childish fit. Once in a while she would look at me and realize she had gone somewhere else in mind. That would upset her and we would usually talk about how the disease was affecting her. For a few weeks this summer she would call me Steven. Steven is my brother with the beautiful operatic voice. 'Steven' couldn't help her dress or assist her in the bathroom. She would get pretty feisty and ask him [me] to leave. One morning, I decided I wasn't going to let her nasty attitude get to me so I started to sing everything I let out of my mouth. I'm not the singer in the family so I know I didn't sound pleasant to her ears. After a time she looked at me and said, *"Well, you ain't no Steven!"* After that when she would think I was Steven I would simply start singing and she would come back to Becky. This month my various personalities seem to have disappeared. I am Becky although who Becky is to her I am not sure. I remain her mainstay no matter who Becky is.

She doesn't smile anymore. That sparkle always present in her eyes is gone. She does laugh if someone else does but it is rare to see a genuine look of understanding of why she is laughing. Larry has always been able to brighten her up but not this month.

She has become increasingly uneasy about where she is. It became hard for her to stay overnight at my sibling homes. She would become very adamant about going home. Sunday dinners at my house had to be stopped. She would be fine for 10-15 minutes then wanted to go home. She gets very angry and manipulative if I didn't take her home right then. When she isn't in her familiar surroundings we have to worry about her wandering away.

There is presently no such thing as changing the subject or getting her redirected. We go through the same routine every evening since November. *"Well, I goofed again." "I'm going to bed."* [Actual time – 3:30 – too early for bed] *"Mother must be worried about me."* These are her statements that always lead to 'going home' questions. *"Where's mother?"* is another constant question.

Her rate of dementia decline has accelerated since October. There seems to be no recall, no cognitive ability, no reasoning. Lying to her has become easier. I don't like lying to her but telling her that mother is at a church meeting helps to keep her calm. Although she doesn't always remember my answers and will keep asking, I have learned she does stay calmer and will busy herself with something if I give her an answer she can identify with. Telling her mother is dead does not calm her it only confuses her. Confusion then creates an angry, edgy mom.

She can no longer dress herself without assistance. A good time passer is simply letting her get herself dressed. When she wants to go to bed at 3:30 I let her go ahead and change into her nightgown. This can take hours and gives her something to do. Tying her shoes is another lengthy ordeal. One day I couldn't find my tennis shoes. She had put them on and had spent so much time getting them tied that it took me 45 minutes to get the knots out of the laces! Yes, I did notice she was tying her shoelaces in knots but I did not realize they were my shoes on her feet. We had identical tennis shoes except for the size. I bought her a pair of tennis shoes with Velcro closures to make the shoe situation easier for her to handle. She cut the Velcro off. Bows or ties on her clothing usually get cut off also. I have hid the scissors but she always managers to find something to cut with.

She has become a neat freak. Nothing can be on the counters or table. She puts dirty dishes away, not necessarily where they belong, but out of sight. One morning the silverware drawer was empty. I finally found it all in the cookbook drawer. It is amazing what you can find around here and in the oddest places. If I try to sew she is constantly picking at my stuff, putting the iron away, pulling the material away as I sew. I have had to replace many needles because of this.

Her fetish for neatness extended to the puzzles we put together over the holidays. I had only a couple pieces yet to fit in one afternoon when the telephone rang. When I got back to the puzzle 10 minutes later she had most of it taken apart and back in its box.

While I was working on Deanna's wedding dress at my house last June mom thought she would help. While I was in the back room pressing a long skirt seam mother used my seam ripper to take apart another skirt seam I had laying by the sewing machine. I put a family movie tape on the VCR to keep her attention off of what I was doing. [Some of my siblings had converted Dads home movies onto videotapes and then dubbed our parents voices in telling who all the people were and what the occasion was. Their grandchildren can also be heard yelling and running in and out of the room as the dubbing was in progress.] Mom was content to watch the tape and soon was talking to it as though she was right there in that time. She would look around to tell the children to quiet down but could not see them. One point of tape moms dubbed voice said "Oh, that's Sally Mae!" In my living room mom said at almost the same time as the tape, *"Oh, that's Sally Mae! Oh, I just said that!"* Luckily I was in the dining room so I could laugh. She has a very hard time distinguishing T.V. from reality. Even the animated

Disney movies are real to her. She does still like watching 'Wheel of Fortune' and can answer most of the puzzles. We watched a movie called '**Jack**'. Several times during the movie she would ask what we were watching. I would tell her the name of the movie and she would then tell me all about her dog, Jack, that she had when she grew up.

Her sleep pattern has changed a lot over the year. For a long time she would awaken every few hours ready to start her day. Then she got to where she would sleep only ½ hour at a time. I tried keeping her awake and active during the day but it didn't help. The more tired she became the more difficult it became to redirect her and keep her calm. The doctor put her on Ambien to help her sleep. After a week trial I discontinued the drug. She would sleep but was always in a drugged daze during the day. I would rather have her cranky and belligerent than like that. Now we are using Haldol. She is sleeping well at night. She still awakens a couple of times during the night to use the bathroom but settles back to bed with no problems. She is alert and not sluggish during the day like she was on the Ambien. Her attitude has improved greatly with the Haldol or is it because she is getting adequate rest again. As we move into this month of January 1999, I am finding I have to wake her up many mornings as she is not waking up as usual on her own. I cut back on the Haldol to see if it makes a difference.

In April she was diagnosed with Congestive Heart Failure and put on Lasix to help reduce the edema. This month the edema has been extreme so the doctor has upped the dosage of Lasix. Yesterday I had to tell the doctor that we would not be doing anything further to stop or try to control the congestive heart failure she is experiencing. Knowing that I have support from my siblings on this matter is helpful yet it does not relieve the fact that I am the one who voiced our opinion to the doctor and made the ultimate decision to not aggressively treat this condition. The right side of her heart is shutting down which is why she is always tired and has so much edema in her legs and ankles. The doctor assured me that mother would probably not have a painful heart attack. She will merely sleep away. Does this ease my pain? No. I find some comfort in knowing that there really is no reason to prolong her life. She really isn't here 90% of the time and even that percentage seems to be shrinking. If mom knew the kind of person she has become she would be mortified. It is also some comfort to know that she will have no pain and simply sleep away. How can they know for sure? How will I feel finding her gone one morning? How will I cope when this happens? I love her so much. I don't want her to die. I didn't want her to get to this point of the dementia. I wanted her to die while she still knew who we were and what was going on. I have mourned over and over as the woman we have always called our Mama, the woman who always gave us nurturing support, who always loved us unconditionally has slipped further and further from us. I have been with her every step of the way in this vicious disease. I have watched that horrible thief steal more and more of her from us. I have tried to love her into staying with us. I can't keep our mother whole. I can't stop this. People say they admire me for staying with her. Many ask why I don't just put her in a nursing home. The answer is I love her. She taught me to love, to hope, to dream, to expect God to always be with me and to always keep God as my leader. She is still teaching me about love. I can do nothing less for her than she would do for me. I don't deny some days are hell and it would be easy to just give up but she needs me. No matter who I am in her mind, my presence still calms her. She taught me to love this deeply; she continues to teach me the power of love. I don't understand why this disease had to become hers, why it had to rob us of our mother and grandmother. Yet, without a doubt I know that there will be something good coming out of this for each of us. We must chose to see what it is and accept it graciously. Many years ago I wrote a poem to her about her. "Look in those eyes. What do you see? I see love and understanding. I see genuine concern for each individual." No longer is that there. There is only confusion, loneliness and fear.

Am I ready? Will I ever be ready to let her go? Please Lord; help me to then rejoice at her release. Thank you Lord, for giving me to her, for helping me find some humor in this pain and for helping me to cope. Carry her home Lord. Release her from this hell.

January 27,1999

Today I met with the staff at EDS. I was very pleased to hear that even though they have noticed a vast change in mother they still see her social abilities as acceptable. She always has appropriate questions for guest speakers who visit. It takes about 10 minutes for visitors to pick up on mom's dementia. She is still cheerful and helps other clients in the mornings. Shortly after lunch she becomes more confused and questions repeatedly how she will get home. They take her for walks if she gets too persistent and they are unable to redirect her thought. Her attention span has diminished markedly this past month. She needs to be directed and supervised while doing craft projects. She can get rather indignant when project time is over and things are cleaned up. She thinks it is all hers and doesn't want it out of her sight. She does appear to be tired more often now but they do not notice any shortness of breath. Three things would have to happen to mark the end of her being allowed to attend EDS. 1- wandering excessively to where a staff person would have to be one on one with her; 2 – needing staff assistance for toileting; and 3 – mean combative attitude

She also enjoys the singing and dancing. The staff had classical music playing while mother was working on her craft item. After about 10 minutes mother related, *"I can tell that is the kind of music that is going to make me want to leave."* Very appropriate response. The music was changed.

Moms mind is pretty good today, more like she was before Christmas.

January 28,1999

Very alert today. Tired, but alert, even more so than yesterday. We had a church ladies luncheon at noon, then grocery shopping and her hair appointment. She did well but was antsy to go home after the lunch and interrupted the meeting frequently by loudly asking to go home. Driving up our lane to the house she mentioned she sure wished dad were still here. I said it was hard to believe it had been almost 7 years since he died and she replied that it didn't seem possible but that so much has happened to her that she is glad he couldn't see her now. She hasn't mentioned our dad for along time, at least not recognizing he has died. Her mind seemed fairly clear all evening. Go figure!

January 29,1999

This whole day she has spent in the total confusion of most of the month of January.

April 1999:

As the days pass it seems there is not much difference in mother's actions yet they are there. She spends more and more time wiping, with an imaginary cloth, the table and counters. This morning she fussed with making her bed for well over an hour. Then after getting all the bedding lined up on one side of the bed she laid down and went to sleep. It takes longer to get her going in the mornings. She doesn't seem to be very 'awake' for a long while after I get her up. Every action has to be explained carefully and deliberately one step at a time. For example: turn on the water – get the washcloth wet- squish out the washcloth – rub your face with the cloth.

She must wear incontinent undergarments now day and night. By taking her to the bathroom every couple hours and not allowing her a lot of liquids in the evening we can pretty much keep this under control. She is beginning to loose control of her bowels also. I must go in the bathroom with her, not so much to assist her but to direct her. She will get detained wiping the counter and sink on her way to the commode and wet herself if not directed. She has to be told where to put the soiled tissue otherwise she will roll it back on the clean roll. Sometimes I'll find it in the towels, in her shower cap, or lined up on edge of the tub.

Showering has changed also. I had been turning on and adjusting the water temperature for her while she undressed then I would make sure she didn't fall stepping into the shower and she could wash herself. Now if left unattended she will only wash the shower walls and not herself.

Much of the time when we need to walk across a parking lot or in a store I have to hold her hand or she will just stop walking. The exception is when we get to the check out counter. She wants to go home not stand there and wait. A tactic she uses now to get me to take her home is to say she has to go to the bathroom. If saying that quietly the first time doesn't get her out of the place she will get louder and louder demanding that she needs to go to the bathroom. She often uses this tactic in church. The minister says he knows when his sermon is boring or too long by watching her.

Unsettled weather creates pacing, constant pacing, can't stop for 1 minute pacing. It is magnified when it gets dark outside.

As I sit here writing this she is once again pulling things out of the hassock and putting them back in. This is a hobby of hers.   Other hobbies include: carrying the sofa pillows around the house and trying to stuff them into the hassock or under the covers of her bed or mine. Turning the water faucets on, taking the nozzles off the faucets, walking up and down the hallway opening and closing all the doors, and changing the shoes on her feet for slippers and back again. Usually she ends up with one of each on both feet. It can be amusing to watch her and try to figure out what is going on in her mind as she does these things. You definitely do not leave anything important in her sight if you want to see it again I now have a hook on my bedroom door to keep her out of there. She can unhook it but it takes her a bit to figure out why the door won't open. I chose not to put a self-locking hook on my door like on the basement door so that I can get in and out quickly.

She sleeps a lot. It is not uncommon for her to sleep sitting up off and on throughout the day. All this daytime sleeping does not interfere with her nights. Usually she will wake up on her own for a bathroom run about an hour after she goes to bed. I get her up at 3:00a.m. to use the bathroom. Most mornings now I have to wake her up. On the days she has EDS I have to start getting her awake for about an hour before I get her up. She likes going to 'school' [EDS] so she tries harder to get motivated.

I try to fill her time with activities that could stimulate her brain. She helps me fold laundry do the dishes and clean. She isn't totally capable of doing these projects but they do provide her with a feeling of usefulness. We play dominoes, put children's puzzles together and while I sew she colors or draws in the coloring books. She can no longer follow the lines for cutting the quilt squares for me but I let her continue to try. I have put together some beautiful quilts from the odd pieces she has cut for me.

So the breakdown now is that she is mentally a 2-3-year-old needing complete help with toileting, bathing and dressing. Yet at times she can converse and respond appropriately. At this point she is actually easier to take care of. Of course, it helps that both of us to get enough sleep at night.

We can watch T.V. again but nothing violent. You just have to be aware that the characters on the television whether real or cartoon are real to her. She can fret over anything she sees for a seemingly unending time. For instance the skating programs; she frets that those children are getting cold outside and I am told to call them in before they freeze. I do wait for a commercial and then change channels with the remote as I leave the room. This usually helps calm her down.

One thing I cannot understand happens on Mondays. Mother can be so totally out of it, constantly changing slippers for shoes and back again or putting her slippers on over her shoes or hiding pillows, asking me where Becky is etc. and yet about noon she starts with the questioning of when I am going to town. Nothing is said all morning about me going anywhere yet she questions when I am leaving. Diane comes every Monday and Thursday afternoon to provide respite care from 3:00 – 10:00p.m. When she comes Mom knows her on Mondays but usually needs to be told who Diane is on Thursdays.

I am leaving Wednesday for a week in Colorado. Susan will stay with Mom while I am gone.

While I was gone Susan managed to convince the rest of our siblings that they needed to visit mom more often. When I returned she reported that each of our sisters had a period of time with mom where they were able to enjoy very lucid conversations. I just couldn't understand how that could be. It had been well over a year since I could say I had a lengthy period of lucid conversation with mom. I didn't doubt them I just couldn't understand it. My turn would come. Before she left Susan told me of a premonition she and our youngest sister had had. They both felt that Dad would come for mother on May 3, the seventh anniversary of his death. That was a bit hard to swallow, what nonsense. I must admit that I watched mom very closely all that day and went to bed that night praying she would still be with me in the morning. As the sun brightened my room I realized I had slept very soundly throughout the night. I hadn't heard mom move all night now I laid ever so still listening for her breathing and praying I hadn't slept thru her passing. I always slept with one ear open like a mother with a new baby. Why had I not heard her during the night? To my great relief I heard her move in her bed. My sisters were wrong!

May 30, 1999

Yesterday Mom was very docile, slow, quiet and slept the majority of the day. I attempted to wake her twice overnight to use the bathroom. She did not respond and her breathing was very shallow. At 9:00a.m. I tried to wake her, again no response. About 11:30 a.m. she started stirring but it still took 15 minutes to wake her fully. Today I literally had to get behind her and move her legs with my legs as I walked. I had to feed her and brush her teeth. Her coloring was ashen and her balance totally off. Total incontinence. Blank stare. Extremely little communication, 1-2 words when she spoke and nothing sensible. Her nose ran all day and she didn't know to wipe it. She slept all day except when I tried to feed her or toilet her.

Did my sisters have the wrong time? Tomorrow would be our parents 52 wedding anniversary. Maybe Dad was coming for her now.

May 31, 1999

I didn't sleep well last night. Mom recognized me this morning but that was the end of anything called awareness. Had to walk her again like I did yesterday. I'm lucky I am so tall and she so short. She fits against me with no awkwardness so I don't loose my balance. I had to spoon-feed her again for breakfast and lunch. She slept most of the day. Bailey, my friend's toy poodle, is with us this week. She has spent much of her day getting up on mom's lap and snuggling, which got mom to petting her. Bailey seems to be awakening mom's senses. I had mom on the toilet and was about ready to give up on getting any results when Bailey came in and insisted on mom petting her. As she leaned forward to pet the wiggling pup she began urinating. She just had to forget herself I guess. Needless to say we repeated that procedure again before mother went to bed for the evening. It worked again. Bailey managed to get mom stimulated enough that she was able to recognize when she needed to use the bathroom again. She was also able to feed herself dinner and brush her teeth when she got ready for bed.

I have taken her off the Haldol as she is not getting agitated towards evening and doesn't need any help sleeping at night.

June 1, 1999

Mom slept well all night and went back to sleep with no problem when I woke her twice for the bathroom. She woke on her own around 8:00a.m. I kept her home from EDS today because she had a grayish ashen tint to her skin last night and was still there this morning. She is very lost and retained that blank stare most of the day. Again she seemed to come out of it by mid afternoon. I believe she is doing well enough that I can go to my own home tonight. Bev will call if she needs me.

June 2, 1999

Bev reported that mom was moving slow but responsive this morning and knew who she [Bev] was.

She asked if she could go to school [EDS] so Bev sent her.

I called EDS to inquire how she was doing. Everything was going smoothly and she didn't appear to have any problems with her heart so I let her stay for the day. When I picked her up this afternoon the girls said she had been happy, smiled a lot and took part in the activities better than she has for the past week or so. They had gone on an outing to a park in the afternoon. Although she was tired she didn't want to leave. The girls had to put her in a wheel chair, as she was too tired to walk. By the time we got home she had that blank stare and no balance. After a trip to the bathroom I sat her on her rocker. She then slept for a little over an hour. After her nap she was more alert and was somewhat able to help me prepare dinner. We had a quiet evening watching 'Wheel of Fortune'. She actually solved 2 puzzles before the contestants did. She was so busy tying Bailey's ears in knots I didn't think she was paying attention to the game show.

Bailey has been very good for mom this week. She follows mom everywhere and likes to be on her lap. Bailey takes such abuse with mom tying her ears together and folding her up. She does jump down when mom tries to bend her backwards. It seems like mom must think that little white thing is a towel. She even tries to pick Bailey up by the fluff on top her head when she is lying on the floor. Bailey yips when her hair is pulled and mom will act surprised that what she touched was a dog. Bailey must like it as she keeps going back for more.

Mother's health continued to decline the following week. She became more and more incoherent, unable to do her own hygiene cares, and she seemed to be in pain from her face, back, chest, and/or constipation. It was not easy to tell where the pain stemmed from because she could not communicate well. Her legs were terribly swollen. She had become very restless and was unable to sleep at night. I needed to prop her up to keep her from coughing so much during the night. She needed assistance to walk because she could not seem to balance herself. Walking produced sweating, shortness of breath and caused her heart to race. Her speech was slurred and mumbled. Now, I was feeding her and reminding her to swallow. Occasionally, I would massage her throat to help her swallow. I believed her heart was failing and that 'her time' was coming soon. It is possible that she may have had a small stroke. I called Hospice and set up an appointment for Monday.

Each night, after putting her to bed, I would read to her, and then we would say our prayers together. I learned there were more verses to the 'Now I Lay Me' prayer than I had learned as a child. "Now I lay me down to sleep. I pray the Lord my soul to keep. If I should die before I wake, I pray the Lord my soul to take. If I should live for other days, I pray the Lord to guide my ways, for I have faith in all you do, show me the way Lord, and I'll follow you. Amen."

The night of June 6, I sat on her bed reading from Joni Eareckson Tada's book, *"**Heaven, Your Real Home**"*. Mom laid there listening with the totally vacant stare I had become used to seeing. After a few minutes, she looked at me with the most radiant smile and fixed clear peaceful eyes on me. *"Now I know God has not deserted me." "I have deserted Him."*

"That's right," I said. "God will never leave his children." We talked for a short while about Gods' abounding love and grace. Then she became quiet and asked when she could go home. I replied, "If you mean your earthly home you are there." "If you mean your heavenly home you only need to tell God you're ready." As I finished speaking that far-away-vacant-stare reappeared in her eyes. Within 20 minutes she gasped and grabbed her chest. Her breathing became very labored and her pulse very erratic. I took her blood pressure; it had dropped. I laid down beside her and held her. I knew she would not be with me in the morning. Through tears of anguish, I said my goodbyes and released her to God's care. I laid by her crying and praying for several hours. Around 2:00a.m. she seemed to be resting comfortably, her breathing more stable.

About 5:30 a.m. I went into the living room. I wrote letters to members of her family to tell them about mom's condition. I had no idea how long she would be with us and I had not written to let them know how she had failed in the past two weeks. As I was getting ready to take the letters out to the mailbox, I heard her stirring and went to check on her. Seeing that she was awake, I told her I would run my letters out to the mailbox before I helped her get up for the day, because the mailman was due any minute. I went out, stuck the letters in the box, put up the flag, and went back into the house. Once at the hallway, I saw her standing at her closet. Surprised to she her up, I asked what she was doing. She replied that she was looking for her clothes, but they weren't in her closet so she was looking on dad's side of the closet. I was baffled. She seemed normal. She questioned where her clothes were and I showed her, but they weren't what she remembered having. Then she had to hurry to the bathroom. I asked if she needed any help and she gave me a look that questioned my sanity as she closed the bathroom door behind her. All of a sudden I heard, *"Rebecca get in here!"* Opening the door I saw her standing in front of the mirror. *"Who is that?"* Now I was totally baffled! Didn't she recognize herself? What was going on? How could she be at death's door the previous night and be walking around this morning as though nothing was wrong with her? She looked at her thin reflection of herself in the mirror. She questioned what was happening to her. If that was Betty, where did all her weight go? She was fat last night, wasn't she? Inquiring what day it was, I told her. With that, she decided she had no more time to waste; we had to get the salads made! Ok, I thought, now she's acting like she has Alzheimer's. I asked, "What salads?"

"For Jerry's party."

"Ok. Whatever," I thought to myself and went to get clean clothes for her to wear. I left her alone to wash and dress while I fixed our breakfast. While we ate, I discovered that my mom was back! Her mind was clearly recalling events that happened six years ago. She was talking about the salads we made for my son, Jerry's, graduation reception. She knew Dad had died, but had no idea that she had Alzheimer disease, that Deanna had lived with her for four years, or that I was living with her now.

What a glorious day we had catching up on all that had transpired the six years she could no longer remember. We went to the beauticians to get her hair done. The girls were stunned by her clarity and enjoyed telling her about all the news around town. My mom, the woman who raised me, was back and was really with me. We talked about the Alzheimer's', how the disease had progressed. She was saddened to learn what had transpired over those lost years, but she wanted to know about everything, including the disease. The day passed much too quickly, and by 8:00 p.m. she started slurring her words again and was having difficulty maintaining her balance. I suggested that she get ready for bed. She did, but didn't want to go to bed. She didn't want to go to sleep; she was afraid she would be 'different' again if she slept. By the time she was in bed, she was incoherent and back to the diseased state. I cannot find words to tell how I felt having my mother back that day. I had nearly forgotten what she had been like before this disease took control of her. I stood by her bedroom door watching her sleep and thanking God for this most wonderful, glorious day. Yes, now I understood the special time my sisters had talked about having with Mom while I was on vacation. Now, *I* had been granted *my* special time. Was this her last hurrah, her rally before death? I cannot explain why, nor do I understand the reason for what had transpired in the past 24 hours...having to cry and release my little mama to God's keeping only one night ago, and then to have my 'whole' mother back for ten hours today? All I could do was say "thank you Lord for your wonderful mercies"!

The next morning she was back in her previous condition and did not recall the events of the day prior. During the next couple of days she regressed to the symptoms she had exhibited the week before 'our reunion' day.

On June 8, the Hospice personnel came out for an evaluation. During their visit Mom slept in her chair but did respond somewhat when they took her vitals. We were now with the Hospice program. They would send someone to help bathe mom in the mornings and feed her breakfast. I felt better knowing I could call them at any time for help. (Is there some law that says, every time you call for help the problem will go away?) Mother improved as the day went on, a friend stopped by for a visit and surprisingly, mom recognized her and carried on a coherent conversation. She didn't need me to feed her for the evening meal and she had become a lot more active. She still needed me to walk with her to provide balance, but a cane would have been sufficient.

I felt Mom was doing well enough that I could leave for a couple of hours, Bev came to sit with her while I was gone. Later, Bev called to say mom had fallen. Mom seemed all right and Bev was using ice packs on her right forearm and forehead. I cancelled my plans and went back to moms.

When I moved to mothers in August 1998, Bev, who was a long time friend of my mother, volunteered to help me care for her. She would pick Mom up from EDS on Tuesday afternoons, take her home and then stay with her until she sent Mom back to EDS on Wednesday mornings. On Fridays, she would pick up mom at EDS and then stay with her until Saturday afternoons. This arrangement worked out quite well for a while, and allowed me time to be with my family. But when Mom started failing so rapidly, I didn't have Bev stay with her anymore; I felt I needed to be with my mom.

Over the summer, my brothers and their families were able to spend some time at the farm with mom and I. Sometimes she knew them, others not. My chances to spend time at my own home were reduced to the hours mom was at EDS and the two evenings each week when my friend Diane would care for mom. This would give me a break from the sun downing routine. It always helped to improve Mom's attitude if someone would stop to visit, even if it was only a few minutes. If I talked on the telephone it irritated her, so calls were kept to a minimum or made after she went to bed. It became a real chore to get both of us ready for church on time. Larry was there some Sunday mornings, and was able to keep Mother occupied while I would get ready and he would keep her from undressing.

At an appointment in July, the doctor could hear damage had been done to mom's heart. She may have had a mild heart attack or an infarct. She has been having more frequent spells with shortness of breath and continued to loose weight. The edema in her legs had not gotten any better. She frequently falls into a deep sleep and her coloring was ashen much of the time.

October 6, 1999

Tonight she is extremely agitated. She is much more argumentative than usual. Finally about 7:15 she sat down and started writing numbers on the hassock and a book.

I spend more and more time retrieving towels, sofa pillows, dishes, you name it. If it's not nailed down it's gone. She is always taking things apart and pulling live plants out of their pots. I can't get her to color in the coloring books anymore but she will color and write on the furniture and walls. Keeping her bed made is a trick anymore. Maybe I should just forget making it each morning and do it just before she goes to bed... although she would probably drag the bedding around the house if I didn't make it. A while back I had to fish one of the sofa pillows out of the toilet so they are all in the basement now. I have told Kathy it is time to take the Haviland china home as mom keeps moving it around. I have retrieved it from the hassock and from under the blankets in the bedrooms. It is not uncommon to find shoes, towels, dirty dishes and even her nightgown in the refrigerator. I have put a latch hook on my bedroom door but she can reach it and get in if she wants to bad enough. She is always on the move and always rambling on about something or counting. Busy, busy, busy. She won't even sit long enough to eat a meal. She likes to move the furniture around and pull the knobs off the stove. I just let her do what ever as long as she isn't getting hurt. I put everything in its rightful place after she goes to bed. I don't dare turn my back to her when she's eating. I did use this time of her eating to take a

128

quick trip to the bathroom but I can't anymore. She has spread butter all over the milk glass or puts the food in her clothes. She has poured her milk in her shoes and smeared her oatmeal in my magazines. One night while we were eating dinner I had to answer the telephone. I was out of the room for maybe five minutes, when I returned she had finished her meal and was nearly finished eating mine. Her clothing can no longer have buttons or embellishments on the front. She will pick and pick until they are off.

Patience and a sense of humor really come in handy. I can see why the caregiver will often die before the patient. The constant repeated questions and the constant rearranging of our environment can get pretty trying on one's nerves. Usually I have no problem dealing with her behavior, but occasionally I have to run out to the garage, around the car and back into the house, to regain my mental balance. If I manage to get into the garage and around the car before the screen door shuts I know I need to go around the car again!

After six weeks, Hospice discontinued their services because mom's condition did not seem to warrant their further need. I could call them when she became worse. Diane still comes two evenings a week and EDS continues to involve mom in their program even though she needs assistance with eating and toileting. They have been wonderful to continue to help me this way. I know I can never express my full gratitude for their caring of mother and me.

October 17,1999

    Today is my birthday and anniversary. I called my husband to wish him a happy anniversary and was talking with him when mom came into the room and asked to whom I was speaking. I told her I was talking to Larry since it was our anniversary. She put one hand on her hip and smartly said in a sarcastic voice, *"Well, bully for you."* I told her it was also my birthday. *"Oh, well, Happy Birthday"* she said sweetly. I asked, "Can you believe 50 years ago you gave birth to me?" *"I did?"* she blurted. "Yes, you did". *"No, Mother is up there,"* she said pointing upward. "Yes, your mother is in heaven but my mother is you," I replied. Very matter of factly she told me I was mistaken, why she had never even been with a man so she could not be my mother. She turned and walked away. I knew she hadn't known me as her daughter for a long time but this cut like a knife into my heart. After I regained my composure I asked, "Mama, don't you remember I'm your daughter?"

    "No, I don't remember much anymore but if I did have a daughter I'd want her to be like you."

    "That's ok," I said. "I'll remember for both of us." I still hurt. My older sister called to wish me a Happy Birthday and I told her what had transpired between mom and I. Kathy wondered if I had found my birthday present yet; I was to look under mom's bed. She talked to mom while I went to find my gift. As I lifted the bed ruffle I saw a large flat box. How did that get there? The end of August I had to make an emergency trip to Colorado. My son was ill and I needed to be with him. While I was gone Susan and

Mom had bought my gift. Susan had wrapped it and placed it under mom's bed. God does work in mysterious ways because many times during the last six weeks I had been down on my knees looking for mom's shoes in that very place and had never seen this beautifully wrapped box. Inside was a beautiful 20"x25" picture of a Victorian woman kneeling in a bed of Iris'. The Bible verse printed on the matting was 1Peter 3: 3,4: 'Your beauty should be that of your inner self, the unfading beauty of a gentle and quiet spirit, which is of great worth to God.' Kathy instructed me to read what was printed on the back of the picture. She told me, "Mom may not know this day who you are but she did the day the picture was bought." I tried hard not to cry as I read the words Susan had printed on the back. - Mama saw this picture at the Christian Book Store and said, 'that looks like your sister Rebecca in my Iris bed...she so reminds me of my mother and the verse fits her so. She has been such a devoted daughter.' – I cried. Somewhere in her mind she did know me as her daughter. Thank you Lord, for another one of your mercies.

I didn't decorate much for Christmas this year as what I did display had a habit of disappearing. Mom had gotten to the point where she didn't know any of her family and was having a hard time of covering her confusion. I volunteered to dog-sit for a friend while she was gone over the holidays. This little dog was the size and color of the little dog I had for 19 years. Ginger, always trying to jump onto Mom's lap, annoyed her for the first few days, but another miracle occurred because of this little pooch. Her presence helped to bring mom out of her fog and she began calling Ginger by my dogs' name. Snooky had died last year. This meant Mom was at least somewhere in the past 19 years. Thanks to this little dog, and the power God worked through her, mother knew most of her children and grandchildren when they were home for Christmas. My brother, sons and their families, arrived Christmas Eve day. Our family tradition was to attend the 11:00 p.m. Christmas Eve church service. Knowing she would not be able to function well for the ritual, mother excused herself after the evening meal to take a nap. Returning from church, mom prepared a salad to be used for the next days' meal. After she went to bed we set up and decorated the tree. The presents were placed beneath the tree. Mother beamed with delight when she woke Christmas morning to find a beautifully decorated tree with gifts under its' boughs. What a blessed Christmas this turned out to be.

January 2000 saw an increase in heart problems and frequent TIA's, which are mini strokes. While eating breakfast, January 29, her hand fell from the bowl to the table. Her eyes were glazed, her breathing very shallow. I tried shaking her arm to snap her out of it but she started tipping over. I carried her to the sofa. She was so pale and her skin so cold. I had called my brother Steven, hoping he could come home. He wasn't able to come, but I was to keep him posted on her condition. This episode frightened me, and once again, I only had God to lean on. Eventually, she started counting but she did not open her eyes, a moment later, she seemed to go to sleep again. Several hours later she started counting again, this time she lifted her fingers, one at a time, and opened her eyes. It took the better part of the day for her to snap out of this episode. This was a day I didn't think I would be strong enough to go through alone, ever again. My husbands shoulder was very broad and comforting that evening.

On April 1st we experienced another of those once-in-a-life-time days. She was constantly on the go but didn't appear to be able to see. She walked across the dining room, taking tiny little steps, while watching her feet. I observed her bump into the wall and thinking she had bumped into someone said, "excuse me", then continued to walk patting the wall as she went along. She could not see to feed herself, so I helped her. In spite of her apparent blindness, she couldn't seem to sit for any length of time. We had Bailey with us again and she followed mom everywhere. With Bailey's company, I actually had a little bit of freedom from mom, she would let me know when mom was into something she shouldn't be. Bailey was getting lots of exercise following mom around. At one point they went into the bathroom where mom managed to open a drawer and pour in a bottle of liquid make-up. While I was cleaning up that mess, she walked into a wall and bumped her head, hard enough this time to warrant an ice bag. I had to sit with her head in my lap so I could hold the ice on her bump. She argued constantly and wanted to get up, so I let her walk. Once again, she patted the walls and furniture to feel her way around. While doing this, she would take pictures off the walls, move the lamps from their stands and lay them on the floor or set them in a chair and open and shut the doors. At one point I asked her to "please sit down for a while"; she did, right on the table where the lamp had been! In another instance, she poked at my foot on the hassock and then tried to pick it up. Once again I asked her what she was doing and she responded, *"The baby is cold so I will throw it away"*. Nothing she said all day made any sense. Then I happened to notice that Bailey wasn't following mom around anymore. Had I put her outside to potty and forgotten to let her back in? No, she would be barking that shrill little bark of hers if she were still outside. I checked all the bedrooms, calling her name all the while I searched. Finally, I heard faint whining; following the sound I opened the hassock and out jumped Bailey! She was so happy to be free to follow mom again. That night, I put mom to bed and Larry joined us as we said prayers. She was forgetting parts of them, but still did very well. Before we finished, she prayed for all of us to be understanding of each other and asked God to bless our lives. She still had her connections with her Lord.

Within the next few days, her sight was fully restored. Evidently, this temporary blindness is a common symptom of Alzheimer disease. It may come and go several times, or it can stay. It can just suddenly stop and never return; Mother never experienced it again.

As April moved along she experienced chest pain more often. One afternoon while feeling her heartbeat, she asked if I could feel anything. I nodded. She replied, *"Good, then I'm still alive."* We shared a good laugh over that.

One evening while I rubbed lotion on her legs, she asked where Becky was. I gave her my best sad-puppy look and asked, "Who am I?"

"Well, you're Rebecca!"

"Yes, I am Becky."

"No, Becky is in the next room," she replied. So, I guess Becky and Rebecca are two different people.

A year earlier, Larry and I planned to take a vacation in May. We wanted to be at my brother Bill's, in Colorado, for his daughters' high school graduation. My other sisters and brother were informed of our plans early enough that they could arrange their schedules to be available for mothers' care. Mother's nieces and nephews planned a big, family reunion at the home place, in Iowa, for Memorial Day weekend. Something inside me kept saying mom had to be at this reunion. I questioned God. How can I possibly take her to this reunion when she needs constant care and doesn't remember anyone? The same answer always came back to me that she had to go. Susan had moved to Iowa, so she and I planned that she would take mom to her home. On Larry's and my way home from Colorado, we would meet at Susan's home and then travel to the reunion together. Two weeks before we were scheduled to leave, Jeanne called to say that no one in the cities would be able to care for mom while we were away. It was suggested that I send mother to EDS everyday, and hire someone to stay with her at night. No. This would not work for me. I insisted that they would have to find a way to share the responsibility so that I could go, or I would not be leaving. I was informed that if they took her and couldn't handle her, they would put her in a nursing home. Kathy, Bill and Jeanne held her health care power of attorney. I knew if they put her into a facility while I was gone, I would not be able to get her out. Family Services helped me arrange a respite stay in the Alzheimer unit at our local nursing home. I was able to use this service for two weeks as respite I would be able to bring mom home after my trip. The little voice in my head kept saying not to do this; she needs to be with family. I tried to call Jeanne, repeatedly, to tell her what I had worked out. She had put a block on her telephone to stop unwanted solicitor calls. I finally was able to reach Deanna and had her call her mother to ask her to call me. By the time she called, I was furious. Now, there was no way I would feel safe putting mom in the Alzheimer Unit. Jeanne was our emergency contact person. If I couldn't reach her, how would the nursing home if they needed too? I told her what I *had* planned to do. I also told her why I had changed my mind. Mother needed to be with family while I was gone; I demanded they make arrangements accordingly. I would drive mom halfway to the cities, Jeanne would meet us and take her from there. I had one week to get mom ready for her two big trips, one to the cities and one to her family reunion. The morning we were to meet, Jeanne called with a change in plans. Kathy would meet us instead of her. Upon meeting Kathy, I asked how she could be there. Hadn't she expected friends from England that morning? Evidently, her friends were not able to come at the last minute, so Kathy was free to help with

Mom. I was very relieved. We transferred the suitcase to Kathy's car and I gave her the care instructions I had written, and the itinerary for our trip. As I put my mama into Kathy's car, I said "good-bye" to her as though I would never see her again. Why? I'd be back; she was in good capable hands. Why had I said good-bye like I did?

As I straightened the house and packed for my trip, I found myself wondering why I hadn't had more patience during the previous week. Mom's constant "Where's Becky", had irritated me to the point that I would have to turn away from her and take a deep breath before I could reply. Aside from her asking that question so frequently, she had not been any different than before. Why didn't I have the patience I normally had? Yes, I needed this vacation with my husband, but I could have postponed it. Why did I feel so driven to be away at this time? Why did I believe so strongly that mom had to go to her reunion? Why couldn't I remain calm and constant with my mother that last week?

I chastised myself the entire drive. By the time we reached Denver, I had the 'knowing feeling' that I would no longer be mom's caregiver when I returned home. Other than that bothering me, vacation was relaxing. When the graduation festivities wound down (May 20), Bill and I stood in his garden looking at the full moon. We commented that our other siblings would really understand now, what it really was like to care for mom during a full moon. The serenity and peace I felt that evening in Bill's garden, clashed with the chastisement I had laid on myself.

On Sunday morning, May 21st, Larry and Jerry went to Grand Junction to go dirt biking; I went with Dan on a horseback trail ride. As we followed the trail up the mountain, and as we were winding back down, I marveled at all God's beauty and remembered my daddy. He and I had often talked about taking a trail ride in the Rocky Mountains. I remember thinking: "Well, Papa, I may not be riding with you on your beautiful Arabians, but I am riding in these beautiful mountains with your namesake. You would be so proud of Dan; he is so much like you."

Driving back to Dan's, we stopped along the Eagle River. We jumped onto a boulder in the river and sat watching the eagles soaring overhead. I unburdened by soul to my son, knowing he would help me sort through my 'whys' and make sense of them. As I stood to jump back to shore, I no longer had the feeling that I would not be mothers' caregiver anymore; I <u>knew</u> I would not be her caregiver again. Just a few hours later, I received the telephone call I did not want.

Mom had a stroke that morning. She was still alive. But why had they waited so long to call me? Jeanne had gone into the bedroom to give mom her medicine and help her get ready for church. Before she would take the medicine, she asked Jeanne if she had done *something* and Jeanne told her "yes". Then she asked if she had done *something else* and Jeanne replied that she had, everything had been taken care of. With that, mom had said, *"my work is done now, it won't be long,"* and then collapsed. Jeanne laid her back onto the bed and called Kathy. They had watched her, not knowing if this was one of those 'spells' I had mentioned, or if she may have had a stroke. Steven

138

arrived after church and assured them this was definitely not a 'spell' as Becky had described them to him. At that point, they called me.

Larry and Jerry had to get back from Grand Junction before I could make plans to return home. I called Bill to tell him about Jeanne's telephone call; she had already called him. Tears prevented us from talking; I would have to call him later.

Kathy called me again to tell me what a wonderful day she and Mom had together Saturday. Mom hadn't seemed to be bothered by the children so they joined Jeanne and her kids for a picnic in the park. She had a wonderful time watching her grandchildren play. Kathy put her to bed that night and after saying prayers, she said, "Mom, you've been a perfect angel today." She replied that she *wanted to be an angel*.

Kathy held the phone to mom's ear so I could talk to her, but she did not respond to my voice.

Larry and I packed up and drove down the mountain to Denver. We planned to pick up Bill and drive home on Monday. Susan called to say she was booking a flight for Bill and me to fly into Minneapolis. We needed to get to the airport, they were afraid we wouldn't get home in time if we drove.

That night as I walked into mother's bedroom, I was taken back by how frail she had become in just one week. My mind flashed back to when I was allowed to see my grandmother the last time. My mama looked just like her mother had on her deathbed. I sat next to her on the bed, kissed her forehead, took her hand and said, "Mama, I'm home." She tried to open her eyes and speak, but could not. I laid next to her with my hand on her chest all night. Steven came in and stayed with us. Her heart stopped. Just as I was going to ask Steven "at what point do the others want to be called in", she raised her arm, with her hand in the 'stop' position, and said "No, No", before dropping her hand. This repeated two more times during the night. Had God said it was time and she was responding "No" to Him?

In the morning, my youngest niece knocked softly on the door. "Aunt Becky, can I come in?" I whispered an affirmative response. She entered, climbed onto the bed and over my side, gently stroked her grandma's face and said, "Grandma, I'm going to school now. I love you. Aunt Becky and Jesus will take care of you while I'm gone. I love you." She left the room and her little brother came in to tell grandma he was going to school also, and would see her when he got home. He went around the bed to speak to her instead of crawling over me like his sister had. These two little people, in all their innocence, with their gentle concern, had unknowingly convinced me that mom needed to remain right where she was until the end.

While I bathed her and rolled her to change the bedding, she opened one eye and glared. Fixing her eye on me, her face softened as though she recognized me. I finished my task and sat to talk to her. "Are you trying to wake up? I'm here now. All your children are here; can you wake up to talk to us?" She gave me a faint smile, and then went to sleep.

I slept with my hand on her chest again that night. This time, the irregular heartbeat she had for years, was not there. Her heart rhythm was regular and surprisingly strong. Around 4:00 a.m. her heart slowed; she seemed to be peaceful. The beat was still steady and regular.

The next morning I told my family what had happened and that her time was very near. I could not stay. I had nothing against the Christian Hymns constantly being played by her bed, or the constant vigil they insisted on keeping at her bedside. I just couldn't go through this part again. Larry and my best friend, Dee, were coming; I planned on going back home with them. Bill also wanted to go to mom's farm, so he planned to go back with us as well. The others were not happy about this. They wanted all of us at her bedside when she crossed.

The family was calmed by Dee's presence; as a nurse she was able to answer their many questions concerning mom. Everything seemed to be falling in place. A minister and dear friend from our childhood finally returned our call. He had been in Romania. An injured thumb brought him back to Minnesota for medical attention. Had he not returned when he did, he would not have known mom was dying. As soon as he was finished at the hospital, he went to Jeanne's. Larry had found our foster sister and told her what was happening. She was on her way. Yes, all the pieces seemed to be falling into place for mom's farewell.

We were finally all together and we gathered around mom and prayed. Susan read a letter that mom had written to all of us in 1996. Slowly, everyone left the room so that those of us leaving for home could say our good-byes.

I sat next to her, holding her hand, caressing her face. Through tears I said, "I'm going home to the farm now, Mama." She grabbed my arm and opened her eyes. She couldn't speak, but her eyes and her hold on my arm, told me she wanted to go with me. "No, Mama, you can't go with me this time. I have carried you this far, now the others need to carry you the rest of the way. You know I can't be here. I need to go home and ready the house for your party. You know who I am, don't you Mama? Thank you for letting me be a part of your life." She smiled her understanding and relaxed her hold on my arm. "I love you, Mama. I'll see you in heaven." She closed her eyes and I kissed her good-bye.

Dee went in next. She said mom had tears in her eyes when she entered the room and sat next to her.

Over the objections of the rest of the family, Bill, Kay and I left that night to go home to the farm.

I think Bill and Kay just needed to touch base with the home place before they could deal with mom's dying. They returned to be with mom late the next afternoon.

I needed to be alone at the farm, to pack up my life there and move it back to my own home. I felt a need to convert the house back to the way it was when Mom and Dad lived there. It needed to be 'their home' when my siblings came again; not mom's and mine. I found a picture of our parents standing in the doorway waving to whoever had taken the picture. They appeared so happy and seemed to say 'welcome home'. I taped it to the door to greet everyone when they came home.

On May 27, 2000, surrounded by the love of her family, Mama died peacefully. It was Memorial Day weekend; 53 years to the Saturday she married Dad. Iris' from her garden adorned the church where friends joined us in the joyous celebration of her life and Home going. We laid her to rest on her actual wedding anniversary, May 31st.

Alzheimer Disease is a debilitating, vicious disease that creates havoc in its victims mind. The disease not only affects the patient but also the family and friends of the patient. It does, in fact, change the lives of all those involved. At times, I wondered if I was strong enough to walk this path with our beloved mother. Patience was never one of my virtues but I learned to be patient as I took this journey. For me, the hardest part was watching the changes that took place in mother. No one likes changes in the familiar; secure places of their life. Accepting these occurrences is difficult for both the victim and the family.

During my childhood, I learned about the faith in God that my parents possessed. While I cared for mother, I learned without a doubt, the deep strength this faith gave mom throughout. It was that faith that made it possible to survive the torments of this disease.

As the disease progressed, mother forgot the place where she was living was the home Dad had built for her. She forgot who her family and husband were. A portrait of my parents hung in her living room, but for almost two years she thought that it was a picture of her parents. The last year, she had forgotten that the

143

rocking chair she loved to sit in had been her grandfathers; she only knew the comfort she felt while in it. I could have moved her to an Alzheimer's Unit, but I would have missed all the glimpses of her past, the mini snips with reality, and the power of faith in her life. I would have missed the little miracles that happened. We all would have missed our last Christmas together. What powerful healing to know that Mama knew her children and grandchildren that last family gathering.

She didn't live in the reality we understood; she felt the familiarity and love that emanated from her surroundings.

I believe the events and the way they played out in May 2000, as well as our entire journey, were all planned by God. My "good-bye" to mom the Saturday before we left on vacation, had to be. My role as caregiver was over. Mom and I had traveled the path God had paved for us. I had gone through the agony of watching her die, all the way down that path, and had done it basically alone. I had to say good-bye to my ward so that I could come back as her daughter. God intended for my family to care for her at the end; not me.

None of us attended the family reunion in Iowa, but we all rejoiced in the wonderful reunion Mother had with her beloved husband, her parents, brothers, and all who had passed ahead of her. *This* was the reunion God had planned.

Regret is an emotion we feel when we look back and see things we should not have done, or things we neglected to do and wished we had done. Regret is not an emotion that I will never feel over my decision to become my mothers' caregiver. I am grateful for the opportunity I was given to care for our Mother.

My life changed through those years. The journey we took together, made my life richer. I learned that the material objects, I once thought so important, are only luxuries of life. Nothing we accumulate in this world can ever be worth as much as the unconditional, self-sacrificing love we give to each other.

Rebecca Clark

ABOUT THE AUTHOR

Rebecca Elizabeth Lowther Clark was born in Iowa in 1949. She was raised in a large, close-knit, Christian family.

Today, Rebecca lives with her husband on a hobby farm near Willmar, Minnesota. In addition to being a wife and mother, she continues to volunteer and devote her time to the elderly.

Her life's journey has presented many challenging adventures. Rebecca has chosen to learn and gain strength despite overwhelming adversity. She is confident that everything has happened for a greater purpose. Clarks gentle humor, sensitivity, and love for her mother comes alive in this wonderful book.